Price Of Fame

A Play by

Charles Grodin

SAMUEL FRENCH, INC.

45 WEST 25TH STREET   NEW YORK 10010

7623 SUNSET BOULEVARD HOLLYWOOD 90046

LONDON   TORONTO

Copyright © 1990, 1991 by Charles Grodin

IMPORTANT BILLING AND CREDIT REQUIREMENTS

All producers of PRICE OF FAME *must* give credit to the Author of the Play in all programs distributed in connection with performances of the Play and in all instances in which the title of the Play appears for purposes of advertising, publicizing or otherwise exploiting the Play and/or a production. The name of the Author *must* also appear on a separate line, on which no other name appears, immediately following the title, and *must* appear in size of type not less than fifty percent the size of the title type.

All producers of PRICE OF FAME must also provide the following billing in any publication or production of the play, on the program's title page or on the page thereafter:

> "Originally produced by The Roundabout Theatre Company, Todd Haimes, Producing Director."

Price of Fame premiered in New York City under the auspices of the Roundabout Theatre Company. It was directed by Gloria Muzio, produced by Todd Haimes, with set designs by David Jenkins, costume design by Jess Goldstein, lighting by Tharon Musser and sound design by Philip Campanella. The cast in order of appearance:

ROGER.............................Charles Grodin
PETE...............................W.J. Paterson
MATT.............................Jace Alexander
MARIO..........................Joseph R. Sicari
KAREN ....Lizbeth Mackay
EVELYN ....Jeannie Berlin
CAPPY...........................Michael Ingram
BOB....................................Sam Groom

CHARACTERS

ROGER CARSTAIRS
PETE
MATT CARSTAIRS
MARIO
KAREN RINGSTAD
EVELYN DUNBAR
RALPH COLEMAN (CAPPY)
BOB LILLKINS

PLACE

The interior of a large, plush motor home.

TIME

The present.

ACT I

7

PETE. (*Surprised.*) Oh, sorry, Roger, I didn't see you come in.

ROGER. That's O.K., Pete. It's dark out.

(*PETE is opening windows, turning lights on, checking the refrigerator, etc.*)

PETE. Sun will be coming up real soon.

ROGER. (*A pause. Skeptically.*) We'll see.

PETE. Anything you need?

ROGER. (*Flat.*) No thanks, Pete.

PETE. (*Cheerfully.*) You've got plenty of juices in there.

ROGER. (*Flat but friendly.*) Thanks, Pete.

PETE. I'll tell everyone you're here.

ROGER. (*Flat.*) Thanks, Pete.

(*PETE goes. ROGER continues to stare at the floor. After a few moments, there's another KNOCK on the door.*)

ROGER C'mon in.

(*MATT CARSTAIRS enters. HE is twenty years old, defensive, explosive, sense of humor.*)

MATT. (*Flat.*) Hi.

ROGER. Hi.

MATT. Want your breakfast?

ROGER. Not now, thanks.

MATT. Want anything?

ROGER. What time did you get in?

MATT. Five.

(*MATT gives Roger a "who needs this" look. A silence— ROGER stares at him.*)

ROGER Do you practice that look?

(*MATT chuckles in spite of himself.*)

ROGER. Ask Mario to come in.
MATT. O.K (*HE goes. Offstage.*) Hey, Mario.

(*ROGER is starting to come-to more. HE now stares
straight ahead. MARIO enters, carrying a makeup kit.
MARIO is in his 50's, a bubbling personality, single-
minded. MARIO crosses D.L. and sets his kit down on
the table.*)

MARIO. I didn't see you come in.
ROGER. That's O.K. It's dark out.
MARIO. (*Chuckling.*) "That's O.K. It's dark out."
Tremendous.

(*MARIO sets up his equipment to begin to make Roger
up.*)

ROGER. (*Rhetorically.*) Mario, where do you go to feel
good? (*ROGER crosses L., sits in makeup chair which is a
director's chair. A pause.*)
MARIO. I go to a place called Geno's, on Melrose. It's
a pizza joint with sawdust and a jukebox. I go there
sometimes after work for a couple of beers, and I feel good.
Ever been there?
ROGER. No.
MARIO. You come with me sometime, you'll feel
good. The picture opens tomorrow, don't it?

(*A long pause.*)

ROGER. Yeah.

MARIO. Oh, I enjoyed it so much. I seen the ad. Looks good. (*A pause.*) Oh, this came last night after you left. (*MARIO reaches over to a counter and hands an envelope to ROGER.*)

ROGER. Oh, this will be the opening day ad in New York.

MARIO. Is it different than L.A.?

ROGER. (*Taking NEW YORK TIMES movie section out of envelope and unfolding it.*) No, but I want to see the placement in the paper. That's important. (*Looking at the ad.*) Oh. No! No!

(*ROGER leaps out of the chair and crosses R. to cellular phone which is sitting on the arm of the sofa D.R. MARIO follows on his heels looking over his shoulder at the ad.*)

MARIO. What's the matter?

ROGER. (*Shocked and upset.*) The horse is in the ad! (*ROGER punches in numbers on the phone.*) How could this happen? There was no horse in the L.A. ad!

MARIO. (*Looking over ROGER's shoulder at ad.*) I like the horse in the ad.

ROGER. Oh no. You don't want the horse in the ad. Believe me! You think people will rush out to see a movie with me and a horse?!

MARIO. Why not? Mr. Ed was very big.

ROGER. Mr. Ed?! This isn't a *talking* horse! (*On phone.*) Is he in? It's Roger Carstairs. (*To Mario.*) *Mr. Ed* wasn't even a movie. It was a TV show. (*On phone.*) Doug, I'm looking at a copy of the *New York Times* ad for Friday. Have you got it? (*A pause.*) I'll hold.

(*There is a KNOCK on the door. MARIO crosses to door U.C.*)

MARIO. I think they made a movie out of it too.

(*A pause. MARIO opens it. KAREN RINGSTAD is standing there. SHE is in her 30's. SHE is attractive, bright, ambitious, vulnerable. SHE carries a manila envelope and a small tape recorder.*)

KAREN.
(*To Mario.*) I'm Karen Ringstad. I have an appointment to do an interview with Mr. Carstairs for *Vanity Fair*.

ROGER.
What's going on, Doug?! The *horse's* in the ad! How could that happen!? Doug, I don't want to believe that somebody deliberately did this.

(*MARIO nods. KAREN enters and watches Roger on the phone. ROGER does not see her.*)

ROGER I know *you* wouldn't do it, Doug. I *know* it's not you. Doug, am I to infer from this that the horse is in all the ads around the country? I *know* it's in not L.A. I *saw* L.A. (*A pause.*) I'd appreciate that, Doug. I'm in my dressing room. As soon as possible, please. Thank you. (*ROGER hangs up the phone and looks at Karen.*)

KAREN. I'm Karen Ringstad from *Vanity Fair*. We have an appointment to do an interview.

ROGER. (*Trying to cool off.*) Oh yeah. Yeah. Right. I forgot. O.K. You want some coffee—anything?

KAREN. No thanks.

ROGER. (*Referring to phone call.*) Did you hear that?

(*KAREN nods. ROGER still filled with agitation.*)

ROGER. This if off the record. O.K.?
KAREN. O.K.
ROGER. Really?
KAREN. Sure.
ROGER. We had a war on this. The studio wanted the horse in the ad—but I don't want that horse!
MARIO. Did you like working with the horse?
ROGER. What?
MARIO. Was he a nice horse to work with?
ROGER. No.
MARIO. No?!
ROGER. (*Shooting Mario a look.*) No, no, he bit me continually.
MARIO. Continually?
ROGER. (*To Karen.*) You may think I'm making too much of a little thing.

(*KAREN just looks at him, noncommittally.*)

ROGER. This happens all the time. You had a picture recently — *Innerspace* — produced by Steven Spielberg — I didn't see it, but I heard it was excellent—excellent. It came out of the chute and dropped through the floor. You got Spielberg and a great picture, it doesn't do business— you start looking around. There's not too many places to look. The ad was ... ridiculous. It was a guy looking at his hand, or something—They put the horse in the ad! (*ROGER sits on the sofa.*)
MARIO. I like the ad with the horse. Look at Clint Eastwood and those chimp movies. The chimp was in the ad too.
ROGER. A chimp isn't a horse!
MARIO. Same thing, Roger. Honestly.

ROGER. (*To Karen.*) Have you seen this picture?

(*KAREN shakes her head "no."*)

ROGER. The horse is a prominent element in the picture.

MARIO. (*Casually, to Karen.*) The horse's great.

ROGER. (*Shooting Mario a quick look.*) But I honestly believe the horse will hurt the biggest job right now, which is getting the people into the theatres in the first place.

KAREN. Why wouldn't the public want to see you with a horse?

(*A pause.*)

ROGER. *Here's* my point! Do you like Woody Allen?

KAREN. Yes.

ROGER. Do you want to see a movie with Woody Allen and a horse?

(*KAREN thinks noncommittally for a moment.*)

ROGER Me neither. And I'll tell you something else, if he ever does a movie with a horse, which I seriously *doubt*—you won't see the horse in the ad! Woody's no fool. (*The PHONE rings.*) Yeah? (*A pause.*) Doug, please make sure that what you're saying to me is 100% absolutely correct. Thank you. (*HE hangs up phone.*) The horse's only in the opening day ad in New York. *Only!* New York is a huge market. It was a mistake by the ad agency. (*A pause.*) Watch, it will do great in New York and die around the rest of the country. (*A pause—HE thinks.*) No way!

KAREN. (*Shaking her head sympathetically.*) A screw-up at an ad agency ...

ROGER. People screw up everywhere. The worst part is how they give the excuse. (*Casually.*) "It was a mistake"—like it was an act of God or something. (*A pause.*) Maybe they should leave the horse in the ad and take *me* out. (*HE smiles.*) It's funny how you can have a sense of humor about something—and still have it eat you up. (*A pause.*) Well, let me get off this. (*ROGER crosses back to makeup chair and sits. Ruefully.*) To sit around worrying if a horse is in an ad or not ... (*Sardonically.*) A mistake. Why don't we get started?

KAREN. All right.

(*A pause.*)

ROGER. Don't you want to turn your tape on?

KAREN. (*Matter-of-fact.*) I had it on when I walked in the door.

ROGER. (*Upset.*) You agreed that everything I've said is off the record.

KAREN. That's right. I won't use it.

ROGER. (*An edge.*) No offense, but I just met you. I'd like you to erase that tape. I mean—I've been carrying on pretty good here.

(*A pause.*)

KAREN. O.K., I understand. (*A pause.*) You want me to erase everything? There was *wonderful* stuff in there.

(*A pause—HE studies her face.*)

ROGER. Like what?

KAREN. How people give an excuse like it's an act of God. How Woody wouldn't have a horse in the ad.

MARIO. I loved that.

KAREN. Great stuff. How you can have a sense of humor about something and still have it eat you up. Smart.

(*ROGER is staring at her.*)

KAREN Funny and human. (*A pause.*) Vulnerable and real.

(*A pause.*)

ROGER. Are you a dangerous character?

KAREN. (*Flashing a winning smile.*) I don't think so.

(*A pause.*)

ROGER. O.K. The hell with it. I don't care. I mean it all, anyway. Let's move on. Why didn't we do this months ago? This piece obviously isn't tied in to the opening of the movie.

(*MARIO continues to apply makeup to Roger.*)

KAREN. I don't think they're looking for a tie-in. This is just about you. Y'know, you get to a certain point where you're bigger than any given movie.

(*HE gives her a suspicious look.*)

KAREN. What's that look mean?

ROGER. It means I'm suspicious of flattery.

KAREN. Don't you think you're bigger than any movie?

ROGER. You hear me talking about the horse, and I think I'm bigger than any movie?

KAREN. Well ... I think you are. (*A pause.*) You're a very big star. You're a household name. There's probably only about ten people as well-known as you are in the movies.

ROGER. Some of the biggest names in Hollywood can't get arrested in the movies today.

(*MARIO chuckles knowingly.*)

KAREN. Who?

ROGER. You're kidding.

KAREN. About what?

ROGER. You expect me to answer that? Roger Carstairs says, "the beloved, legendary so-and-so can't get arrested in the movies."

MARIO. That's all you need.

ROGER. What kind of an interview is this?

MATT. (*Sticking his head in door.*) Dad, they need you for a lineup.

(*ROGER gets up. MARIO follows.*)

KAREN. Your son works on the movie?

ROGER. Yeah.

KAREN. You're divorced, right?

ROGER. (*Noting her casualness.*) Right.

KAREN. What's a lineup?

(*ROGER rises and crosses to her.*)

ROGER. (*Drily joking.*) Sometimes something will happen on the lot—a purse-snatching—something like that, and security puts out the word to round up all the usual suspects for a lineup.

(*SHE stares blankly at him.*)

ROGER. It's a lighting lineup. The cinematographer wants to see exactly where we'll be in a scene. Feel free to call New York, your broker—whatever. (*Hands her phone.*)
KAREN. I *have* a broker.
ROGER. (*Crosses to door.*) I'm sure.
MARIO. (*Exits; chuckling.*) "All the usual suspects." Tremendous.
ROGER. (*As HE goes.*) I won't be long. There's juice in the refrigerator. Help yourself. The piece of fudge on the second shelf is off limits. *I'm* going to eat that. (*A pause.*) That's a joke. There is no fudge. Completely forget I said that. (*HE goes.*)
KAREN. (*Stands there a moment and thinks. Then SHE dictates.*) A horse in the ad or no horse in the ad—that is the question. At least it seemed to be the morning I arrived for my meeting with Roger Carstairs in his sumptuous movie star motor home. Carstairs was on the phone screaming at an ad agency in New York. A photograph of the horse in his movie, *That Town,* had appeared, by mistake, in a full-page ad in the *New York Times* and Roger was in a frenzy about it. A horse in an ad or no horse in an ad might not seem to rank up there with "To be or not to be" as a pressing question, but to Carstairs it took on proportions of life and death. (*A pause. SHE thinks.*) Carstairs, for years, has consistently ranked as one of the top ten most popular movie stars in this country, but popularity doesn't always translate into box office success, and the failure of Carstairs' last four

pictures—(*To self.*) Check exact titles and dates—have not only put his bankability as a major box office star into serious question but possibly even his popularity itself. Carstairs is a movie star on the ropes, and he acts like it. (*SHE clicks off the tape. SHE stands there a moment—then goes to the phone.*) Hi. Any messages? Uh huh, uh huh. Right. I'm, uh, in Roger Carstairs' motor home. Fine. He's ... interesting. I'm just not really crazy about the angle. I mean, Bob comes up with a headline—"What's wrong with Mr. Right?" To us it's an interesting angle for a piece on someone who's always gotten good press. To him, it's going to be a hatchet job. That's *not* too strong a word. That's what Bob wants. A hatchet job.(A pause. With determination.) No, I'm *doing* it. Of course, I'm doing it.

(*EVELYN enters. SHE is in her 40's, insecure, appealing and compassionate. SHE speaks somewhat rapidly.*)

EVELYN. Roger?

KAREN. (*On phone.*) I'll check with you later. Bye. (*To Evelyn.*) He went to the set. They're doing a lineup.

EVELYN. (*Dealing with her insecurity of being left out.*) I'm Evelyn Dunbar.

KAREN. I'm Karen Ringstad. I'm doing a piece on Roger for *Vanity Fair*.

EVELYN. Oh. I play Roger's wife in the movie.

KAREN. What's he like to work with?

EVELYN. I love Roger.

KAREN. What's the best thing about him?

EVELYN. (*Quickly.*) He's a great guy. We were in acting class together in New York. I dropped out of the business for a long time and had my babies. Then when I wanted to get back in—I called Roger, and he recommended me to the director. I auditioned and I think I got it because

Roger wanted me. You know what's the best thing about Roger? He's the only person I've ever known who got famous and didn't change. He's the same guy. You never see him acting like a star.

KAREN. You don't find him sometimes neurotic and obsessive?

EVELYN. He was like that as an unknown. He cares about everything a lot, so he thinks about everything a lot.

KAREN. Is there a specific incident you can remember that would show him, when you were all starting out, being neurotic or crazy, or whatever—?

EVELYN. (*A pause as SHE thinks.*) Well ... what comes to mind right away when you ask that—a specific incident ...

KAREN. Yes.

EVELYN. I was with Roger and a couple of us were coming out of class one day, and a few guys were standing on the corner—New York, y'know...

KAREN. Yes ...

EVELYN. And one of them said something pretty rough to one of the girls—"I'd like to ..." y'know. Roger walked over to the guys and asked, "Who said that?" One of them said "I did," and before he finished the word "did," Roger knocked him out. He knocked him out with one punch.

(*A pause.*)

KAREN. What did the other guys do?

EVELYN. Nothing. Everybody just stood there for a second, and then Roger just walked away with us.

(*MARIO enters.*)

MARIO. Oh hello, Miss Dunbar, how are you today?

EVELYN. Fine, Mario. They weren't looking for me on the set, were they?

MARIO. (*HE powders her nose as he passes and crosses L. to his makeup kit.*) No.

KAREN. Mario, what's Mr. Carstairs like to work with?

MARIO. Roger? He's a regular guy. He's like a person.

KAREN. How long have you been making him up?

MARIO. Over twelve years.

KAREN. Do you have a story where Roger was ... more like a regular movie star—instead of a regular person—where he was ... different than he usually is ... in some way.

MARIO. No.

KAREN. No?

MARIO. Roger's always like he is. He's like Roger.

KAREN. And you like him.

MARIO. C'mon!

KAREN. What?

MARIO. I love him!

EVELYN. (*To Mario.*) That's what I said.

MARIO. Why not!?

ROGER. (*Enters. To Evelyn.*) Hi. (*HE pats her shoulder.*)

EVELYN. Your ears must be burning.

ROGER. (*Indicating Karen.*) You've met?

EVELYN. (*Nods "yes".*) I was just telling the story of that time you punched that guy out who said that thing to June.

ROGER. (*Smiling.*) That's when I was in my prime. (*A pause.*) I've got a better story. This happened about ten years later. (*A pause, thinks a moment.*) I was going into that restaurant on the Upper West Side—what's it called— the Library restaurant. Remember that?

EVELYN. Sure.

ROGER. It's gone now. I'm walking in there with Eleanor Kellerman ...

MARIO. Eleanor Kellerman. Oh, she's beautiful.

ROGER. And a guy sitting at the bar makes one of those sounds—you know how guys do with their lips—

(*HE makes a loud kissing sound.*)

MARIO. Oh, I hate that.

ROGER. Worse than that. Awful. I just lost it. I ran over and grabbed him and said, "What the hell are you doing?!" The guy stands up, and he was a real moose— you couldn't really tell while he was sitting—He grabs my wrists and says, "Why don't we step outside." Well, I see right away he could kill me—I mean, *literally,* but I don't want to back off—so I say, (*Very aggressively.*) "Nobody's steppin' outside! *Nobody's steppin' outside!*"—like I was the police, or something.

MARIO. (*Chuckling.*) What'd he do?

ROGER. Well, he was confused, because he thought *he* was the tough guy, but I was acting like *I* was. All this time I'm acting tough—he's squeezing my wrists harder—I mean the skin broke,—I felt like crying, but I'm just acting tougher. (*To Karen.*) Everyone's life story.

(*KAREN makes a note of Roger's last line. HE looks at her.*)

EVELYN. So, what happened?

ROGER. Thank God, somebody jumped in and broke it up. As they pulled me away I did one of those (*Shouting.*) "Let me at him" moves. I wanted to leave, but Eleanor wanted to stay, so we stayed. It was very ... (*Remembers unpleasantness.*) I never went in there again.

KAREN. Were you a fighter?

ROGER. No ... just a bad temper.

KAREN. Do you still have it?

ROGER. (*Considers it.*) I don't know. I haven't been that provoked in a long time.

(*A silence.*)

EVELYN. You want to run the scene?

ROGER. Yeah. Good.

MARIO. I've got a little more work to do on you.

ROGER. O.K.

(*HE crosses L. and sits in the director's chair. MARIO works on him through the following.*)

MARIO. "Nobody's steppin' outside! *Nobody's steppin' outside!*" Tremendous! (*MARIO chuckles appreciatively.*) You ought to do those kind of parts.

ROGER. (*Dismissing the idea.*) That was a long time ago, Mario.

MARIO. Ah, you could *still* do it!

ROGER. (*Chuckling, to Evelyn.*) Let's run it.

EVELYN. O.K. I'll pick it up with—"You can't go—I'm afraid."

ROGER. O.K.

(*THEY run the lines speedily but somewhat perfunctorily, really more for sense than a lot of expression.*)

EVELYN. "You can't go—I'm afraid."

ROGER. "Look, there's something out there."

EVELYN. "Mark, I'm afraid. Don't do it. Let it call to you—at least." I don't really understand that line—"Let it call to you—at least." Does it mean if the creature makes its sound—it would be O.K. with her if you went out?

ROGER. If the creature calls, at least it's reaching out.

EVELYN. How do we know that? A creature's sound doesn't necessarily mean it's reaching out. It can mean it's warning you to keep away.

ROGER. That's a good point.

EVELYN. I mean, later we learn it's reaching out—but now we don't know that. You don't really know *what* a creature's sound means, until you're with the creature.

MARIO. That's true. My dog, Boy, makes the most growling sound, but when you're with him—he's the nicest dog.

ROGER. You have a dog named Boy?

MARIO. Yeah. I couldn't think what to name him. I couldn't make up my mind between Rex and Fido.

ROGER. You considered Fido?

MARIO. (*With intensity.*) Yeah, Rex, Fido, Rex, Fido, Rex, Fido. I thought I was going crazy ... and while I was trying to decide, I'm saying, "Here, boy, here, boy" ...

(*A pause.*)

ROGER. (*Laughing.*) Where were we?

EVELYN. "Let it call to you, at least." I'll discuss the line with Jay, but let's keep running it. "Let it call to you, at least."

ROGER. (*Quickly.*) "Doris, there's something there. I'm *not* afraid. I'm excited. Sometimes we don't *know* what's there but we go anyway, because not to would feel worse. After all, it's not every day that a creature from another world shows up in your back yard. Of course, if it turns out to be too tough, I'll be back before the screen door closes." See, I think that last line is too much of a joke.

EVELYN. Oh, I love that! It's so charming after all the heroic stuff, for you to have a human moment like that.

ROGER. (*To himself.*) "Of course, if it turns out to be too tough, I'll be back before the screen door closes."

(*A pause. MARIO chuckles.*)

ROGER. Yeah. Yeah. O.K. Good. 'Cause that's what people do when they're nervous—they joke, whether it's about creatures from outer space, or what.
EVELYN. That's a great line.
MARIO. Oh, no question about it.
ROGER. O.K. Good. I don't know when we'll get to this. He seems to be shooting some special effects stuff. So, maybe not till tomorrow—but we'll run it again, before we do it.
EVELYN. Good. And I'll speak to Jay about that line. (*EVELYN rises and crosses U.C. to door.*)
ROGER. O.K. Good. (*Turning to Karen.*) I've been ignoring you.
KAREN. That's O.K. I've been taping this.

(*EVELYN stops.*)

ROGER. (*Taken aback.*) You've been taping this?!
KAREN. My tape recorder is always on.
ROGER. (*Edgy.*) Well, please let's make it that your tape recorder is always *off*, unless you *tell* me it's on. We're not doing a documentary.
KAREN. I'm sorry.

(*KAREN crosses R. to sofa and sits.*)

ROGER. This is the way you always work?
KAREN. Yes.
ROGER. And no one objects?
KAREN. Sometimes people object.

ROGER. (*Cynically.*) If they're aware of it.

KAREN. I think if a reporter walks in a room with a tape recorder, people should realize they're being taped.

ROGER. (*Frustrated.*) A reporter! You're not here to do a news story.

KAREN. In a way, I am.

ROGER. (*Looking to Evelyn and Mario.*) Boy, I don't know. Am I crazy? Am I overreacting because I have a horse in my ad?!

EVELYN. (*To Roger, reassuringly.*) You didn't say anything you'd mind seeing printed.

ROGER. Really?

EVELYN. Really. (*SHE crosses D.R. to Karen.*) I don't think you need to keep it on when we're running the scene, though.

ROGER. Right.

EVELYN. Because I'd hate to have anyone hear us doing it *that* way.

ROGER. Right.

EVELYN. Because we're not really *doing* it.

ROGER. That's right.

KAREN. No one will hear it but me.

ROGER. (*Edgily.*) How do we know that?

KAREN. (*Looking him straight in the eye.*) Because I'm telling you.

ROGER. Mario, you find this strange?

MARIO. (*Completely lost.*) What?

(*A pause.*)

ROGER. Never mind. O.K., looks like I've got some time now, so ... (*To Karen, edgily.*) Why don't we do the interview.

(*There's an uncomfortable silence in the room.*)

EVELYN. O.K. I'll speak to Jay about the line. (*To Karen.*) Nice to have met you.
KAREN. Thanks. Same here.

(*EVELYN exits.*)

MARIO. (*Leaving.*) I'll be on the set if you need me.
ROGER. O.K. Thanks, Mario.

(*MARIO exits.*)

ROGER Is the tape recorder on or off?
KAREN. Off. I turned it off when you got mad.
ROGER. You think I have a right to be mad?
KAREN. I can see your point. I don't agree with you, but I can see your point.
ROGER. (*Crosses R. to sofa.*) And you don't agree with me, because you see yourself as a reporter doing a news story? A *news* story, not an interview?
KAREN. An interview with you could easily be news. You're a man who's famous all over the world.
ROGER. I'm a man who just made a movie with a horse. That's news?

(*HE amuses himself with the description, and begins to relax. HE sits in the easy chair D.C. A pause.*)

KAREN. (*Very friendly.*) Can I put the tape recorder on?

(*A pause.*)

ROGER. Put it on.

(*KAREN takes an old clipping out of her envelope and puts the recorder on.*)

KAREN. I want to read you something from an interview you gave last year. O.K.?

(*Hesitantly; ROGER nods.*)

KAREN. (*Reading from article.*) "I think life is about making a difference—that the world should somehow benefit in some tiny way from my having passed through. If people could feel good about having come into contact with me, that would mean something."

(*ROGER squirms uncomfortably. KAREN sees this.*)

KAREN. You seem uncomfortable. Why?
ROGER. I really don't like to hear myself quoted.
KAREN. Why not?
ROGER. The part of me that doesn't like myself wants to yell, "Shut up!"
KAREN. Why doesn't part of you like yourself?
ROGER. Because I'm human.
KAREN. You think every human in some way dislikes themselves.
ROGER. Yes.
KAREN. Why?
ROGER. (*Figuring it out, as he speaks.*) Because we aspire to be perfect, but by nature we're not, and I think the inevitable failure leads to at least some amount of self-loathing. (*A pause. He smiles to himself.*) Pretentious enough for you?
KAREN. (*SHE stares at him a moment—thinking about what he's just said—then looks at her quotes.*) "As far as I'm concerned, the degree you can have feeling for

things outside of yourself is your measure as a person. It's amazing how few people can feel anything outside of their self-interest." (*SHE puts article down.*) Don't you think you sound like a do-gooder?

ROGER. (*Real curiosity.*) When did doing good get to be a bad thing?

KAREN. (*Smiling at him.*) You think the degree of self-interest has risen?

ROGER. Don't you?

KAREN. I don't know ... *Time* or *Newsweek* had a cover story saying greed is out for the '90's.

ROGER. (*Chuckling sardonically.*) Oh, then it must be.

KAREN. (*Looking at article.*) Have you made people feel good about coming into contact with you?

ROGER. (*Smiling.*) Present company excluded?

KAREN. (*Smiling.*) Have you?

ROGER. You'd have to ask people who come into contact with me.

KAREN. I have.

(*ROGER looks at her.*)

KAREN. You're doing fine. Don't you sound a little too good to be true?

ROGER. Yeah.

KAREN. Are you?

ROGER. Yeah.

KAREN. Yeah, what?

ROGER. Too good to be true.

KAREN. So there's another side. The imperfect side, as you would put it.

ROGER. You might say so.

KAREN. What's that about?

(*A pause.*)

ROGER. I like anchovies.

KAREN. (*Laughs.*) Would you like to get on a lighter note?

ROGER. (*Laughing.*) Please. (*HE crosses U.C. to the coffee which has been brewing.*)

KAREN. How do you feel about being famous?

ROGER. That's lighter?

KAREN. A little.

ROGER. You want some coffee or anything? (*HE pours coffee.*)

KAREN. No thanks.

ROGER. I don't know. After a while, it's just you.

KAREN. So?

ROGER. I guess you get used to being treated better than the average person. I once heard someone very well-known say that when he was doing great—it was "yes, yes, yes," to this, to that—on the cover of everything, and then one day there was one tiny "no," and it was shattering.

KAREN. Who said that?

ROGER. It was in a private conversation.

(*A pause.*)

KAREN. He meant when the music stops?

ROGER. Yeah.

KAREN. Do you worry about that?

(*A pause.*)

ROGER. Not the way a lot of people do. (*A pause.*) I never had the big ride on the yesses. I never got all tingly from a standing ovation.

KAREN. You've had standing ovations?

(*A pause. HE stares at her.*)

ROGER. (*Easily.*) I've done a lot of theatre.
KAREN. I know, but I thought standing ovations were pretty unusual in the theatre.
ROGER. (*Ironically.*) I got them.
KAREN. Did I offend you just now?
ROGER. (*Staring at her.*) Are you trying to?
KAREN. I don't think so.

(*A pause. HE crosses and sits in easy chair D.C.*)

ROGER. When the music stops. That's a price of fame.
KAREN. (*Taking a note.*) Price of fame. That's good. That's a good title for this piece. (*A pause.*) So tell me about the price of fame.
ROGER.(*Subtly teasing.*) Well ... you have to talk to people who are more interested in titles than in you.
KAREN. I'm interested in you.

(*There is a silence as HE looks at her.*)

KAREN The price?

(*A silence.*)

ROGER. What's the price of anything? I had a terrible experience once and met a best friend. What's the price? You break a leg and marry your nurse, but get a divorce. What's the price? They throw tomatoes at you, and you acquire a taste for vegetables. You live longer, but maybe you don't want to.(*A pause.*) Maybe we don't know the price of anything until our lives are about over.

(*A pause. From outside the motor home there is a loud, high-pitched SOUND: Be be be be be. RALPH COLEMAN [CAPPY] enters, carrying a puppet. CAPPY is 40's, outgoing, clever, vulnerable, an explosive, exuberant sense of humor. We see the PUPPET first appear in the doorway. The PUPPET sees Roger—then Karen—then recoils in mock horror.*)

CAPPY. (*Using high-pitched voice of puppet.*) Roger! You said we were engaged! Who is this woman?!

ROGER. (*Without turning around. Chuckling.*) This is Karen. She's doing an interview, but she'll turn her tape off now.

(*HE gives her a look, and SHE does.*)

ROGER. This is Cappy.

CAPPY. (*Creature sound.*) A pleasure to make your acquaintance. (*HE extends creature's hand to shake KAREN's hand.*)

KAREN. How do you do?

ROGER. Cappy does the voice of the creature.

CAPPY. (*As creature.*) Be be be.

ROGER. They use a mechanical creature, large puppets. What else?

CAPPY. (*As creature.*) I have no idea.

KAREN. You work the puppets?

CAPPY. (*As creature.*) No, he just acts. He carries me when we run lines, 'cause he feels silly.

ROGER. Of course he feels silly when he *doesn't* run lines, too. Let's run it. "I'm coming out. I want to speak to you."

CAPPY. (*A high-pitched sound, as creature.*) "Be be be be be be be." (*To Karen, own voice.*) That's my other-world sound.

KAREN. (*Laughing.*) It's great.

ROGER. "I'm friendly. We want to help you."

CAPPY. (*Creature's voice.*) "We want to help you."

ROGER. "Help us with what?"

CAPPY. (*Kidding, with creature's voice.*) Help you get smarter. You're pretty dumb to be in a movie like this.

ROGER. (*Laughing.*) We'll never get through this.

(*MATT knocks on the door and sticks his head in.*)

MATT. Mr. Coleman, we'll be ready for you in five minutes. (*MATT goes.*)

ROGER. "What do you want? How can I help you?"

CAPPY. (*Crosses L. of Roger. As creature.*) "Tell others we are here. Tell them to come to the park by your observatory after dark."

ROGER. "Griffith Park?"

CAPPY. (*Teasing, as creature.*) Yes, putz. Want me to tell you what bus to take?

(*THEY ALL laugh.*)

CAPPY (*As creature.*) "Tell those who would try to capture us—they cannot."

ROGER. "Yes."

CAPPY. (*Kidding, as creature.*) And on your way over pick me up a corned beef sandwich on a seeded Kaiser roll with Russian and a slice of tomato with a side of fries.

(*THEY ALL laugh.*)

ROGER. Anything to drink?

CAPPY. (*Creature's voice.*) A diet Pepsi with a twist of lime and two straws. I'm sharing it with my niece.

KAREN. (*Still laughing.*) Oh God, I've got to use the bathroom.

ROGER. (*Pointing toward sliding door.*) Through there.

(*SHE enters bedroom and goes into bathroom. ROGER crosses to a counter on the back of the sofa and picks up a manila envelope.*)

ROGER How much longer do you have on the picture?

CAPPY. (*Pours himself some coffee.*) A couple of months—why?

ROGER. Book sanitarium time.

CAPPY. (*Laughs. As creature.*) I already have.

ROGER I want you to see the ad for my new movie and tell me where your eye goes first.

CAPPY. (*As the creature.*) Which eye?

(*There are two envelopes lying on the table. ROGER has reached into Karen's manila envelope which is identical to his, by mistake. HE pulls out a handful of old clippings and a sheet of paper with notes. About to put it back.*)

ROGER. Oh, this is Karen's stuff.

(*Suddenly his eye catches something that's written on her page of notes. HE is absorbed by what he sees. HE stares a moment toward the bathroom, clearly upset. After a moment, HE puts her notes back. Through this, CAPPY has been looking through the refrigerator.*)

CAPPY. How *is* the movie? I haven't seen it.

ROGER. (*Distracted, but trying to conceal it.*) Good.

(*ROGER finds the ad in his envelope and takes it out. CAPPY crosses to Roger and takes ad from Roger.*)

CAPPY. The horse. My eye goes right to the horse. It's a *talking* horse—right?

(*ROGER is just staring, not smiling. CAPPY sees this quickly.*)

CAPPY (*Supportively.*) Mario told me what you were worried about. If it's a good picture, people will go to see it. Don't worry about the horse.

(*ROGER nods. MATT KNOCKS and sticks his head in.*)

MATT. (*To Cappy.*) They're ready for you.
CAPPY. I'm outta here. A short scene, and then I'm meeting with my banker. (*As HE moves toward door; creature's voice.*) Give me your money, or we will get you with droppings from outer space. *Droppings From Outer Space* at theatres everywhere—Senior citizens discount. (*As the door closes, we hear.*) Be be be be be be be.

(*ROGER stands there. HE's still preoccupied. After a few moments HE crosses to the director's chair—sits and just stares. After a moment, KAREN comes out of the bathroom.*)

KAREN. (*Looks around.*) Oh, he left. He's funny. He's so clever. (*SHE becomes aware that ROGER is just staring at her.*) Is everything O.K.?
ROGER. (*Matter-of-fact.*) Yeah.

(*An uncomfortable silence.*)

KAREN. Did something just happen?

ROGER. Why do you ask?

KAREN. I was only gone for a minute. When I left, you were in such a great mood.

ROGER. He had to go to the set.

KAREN. Oh. And now you're stuck with me. (*A pause. SHE moves toward him with her tape recorder.*) Are you angry about something?

ROGER. Why don't we move ahead without the tape recorder? People are in and out of here, and I don't want to have to watch you to see if it's on.

(*A pause.*)

KAREN. You're still mad about the tape recorder? I thought you were over that.

(*HE stares at her. SHE crosses R. to sofa.*)

KAREN. (*Attempt at humor.*) Maybe I ought to have Cappy sit in on the interview to keep you in a good mood.

ROGER. (*HE just stares.*) Why don't we move ahead?

KAREN. (*Realizing SHE's getting nowhere in improving his mood. There is considerable discomfort.*) O.K.(*A pause.*) No tape recorder. I'll just take some notes, O.K.?

(*ROGER stares. A pause.*)

KAREN. Cappy said you were pretty dumb to be in a movie like this. Was that a joke?

(*A pause.*)

ROGER. (*Edgily.*) I hope so.

KAREN. What do you think of this picture?
ROGER. I hope to help make it as good as it can be.
KAREN. You didn't answer the question.

(*A pause.*)

ROGER. (*HE stares at her.*) I liked it enough to agree
to do it.
KAREN. (*SHE crosses C and sits.*) So ... no regrets?
ROGER. You mean in life?
KAREN. O.K.
ROGER. I have regrets in life.
KAREN. What would you do differently?
ROGER. I'd try not to make any mistakes.
KAREN. What mistakes did you make?

(*HE stares at her. SHE gets increasingly uncomfortable.*
HE rises and crosses to her.)

ROGER. I think the biggest mistake a person can make
is doing something that can affect your opinion of
yourself.

(*A pause.*)

KAREN. Can you give me an example?

(*A pause.*)

ROGER. Going along with things that are wrong. Not
speaking out.
KAREN. About what?

(*A silence*)

ROGER. (*HE stares at her. Pointedly.*) You really can't get away with doing something lousy if you are a person of conscience. Are you a person of conscience?

KAREN. Well ... yes.

(*SHE stares at him. There is a KNOCK on the door and MATT sticks his head in.*)

MATT. Jay wants you on the set.

ROGER. Am I shooting something?

KAREN.(*SHE rises and crosses R. Ironically.*) Just me.

MATT. No, he just wants to see you for a minute.

ROGER. (*Stares at her.*) I'll be back.

KAREN. (*Appreciating the reprieve.*) Take your time.

(*ROGER goes. KAREN sits on the sofa thinking about what's just happened.*)

KAREN (*SHE picks up the phone and punches in a number.*) Hi. Anything? Uh huh, uh huh, uh huh. Did she leave a number? Uh huh. (*Makes a note. A pause.*) Oh, put him on. Hi, Bob. Fine. Uh ... No, I'm *still* not that comfortable with the angle. I *am* doing it. He's pretty sharp, though. Well, I mean you can't ask him, "Did you ever kick your dog?" Have you met him? Well, you seem to have your teeth into going after him so much—I just suddenly wondered if there were anything personal. I'm not attacking you. I was just asking a question. I'm *not* attacking you, Bob. I *am* being respectful. Yes, Bob. Yes, Bob. Uh huh. Uh huh. Yes, Bob. Yes, Bob. I'll ask him. (*Makes a note.*) He's, uh ... very forthcoming. I think it will be a good piece. I don't know. Why don't we play it by ear? This may take more time than I thought. No, it's just ... there's a lot of stuff. O.K. I'll talk to you later. Bye. (*SHE puts down the phone and suddenly seems tired.*

SHE looks around the motor home, checks her notes, picks up the phone.) Andrea?! Hi. Karen—I just picked up your message. Guess where I am? Roger Carstairs' motor home—some bedroom in here—Between us—Bob wants me to do a hatchet job on him—Well, he's always gotten great press, and there's got to be another side. Sure, it's legitimate. (*A pause.*)—It's not writing lies—if we have a problem doing anything else—we shouldn't be in the business—Right? Exactly.

(*ROGER enters.*)

KAREN. I better get off. I'll call you later. Uh, uh. I'll just talk to you later.

(*HE stands U.C. and stares at her. SHE hangs up the phone. SHE checks her face in her compact and begins to reapply some makeup.*)

ROGER. (*A little more relaxed—but still on edge.*) Want me to have Mario take a look at you?
KAREN. (*Looking up at him.*) Do I need it?

(*There is a moment as THEY stare at each other.*)

ROGER. You're fine. (*A pause.*) So what are your flaws?
KAREN. Physical or character?
ROGER. We were talking about character.
KAREN. You're unrelenting.
ROGER. So are you. (*A pause.*) You married?
KAREN. I'm engaged—I guess you could say...
ROGER. When are you getting married?
KAREN. We haven't set a date, exactly ...
ROGER. (*A pause.*) Why not?

(*SHE stares at him.*)

ROGER. Too private?
KAREN. No, I just didn't want to use our time talking about myself.
ROGER. Have you got a time problem?
KAREN. Not really. Do you?

(*HE crosses and sits on sofa about two feet from where SHE is sitting.*)

ROGER. No, you can hang around getting your dirt, as long as you like.
KAREN. (*Uneasily.*) Dirt?
ROGER. (*Shrugs.*) Figure of speech. Info.

(*KAREN nods uncertainly.*)

ROGER. So why haven't you set a date?

(*A pause.*)

KAREN. O.K. I'll make a deal with you. I'll tell you my story if you tell me yours. Who you *really* are—like you were doing before—there was good stuff in there.
ROGER. (*Easily.*) Think you can dig it out from all the crap?
KAREN. I didn't mean it that way.
ROGER. O.K. I'll take your offer. (*A pause.*) So why haven't you set the date?
KAREN. O.K. And then you're going to be forthcoming.
ROGER. Oh, I'll probably be more forthcoming than you can use.

KAREN. That sounds good. I haven't set the date, because I'm not 100% sure I want to marry the man.

ROGER. What's his name?

KAREN. Bob.

ROGER. What's he do?

KAREN. He's my editor.

(*A pause.*)

ROGER. (*Seems to come to a realization. A pause.*) What's the problem?

KAREN. It's a relationship, y'know ...

ROGER. Not really. There's all kinds.

KAREN. Well ... we have a good kind.

(*ROGER nods—a pause.*)

ROGER. Would you be happy with these answers from me?

KAREN. No. Am I making you unhappy?

ROGER. I don't know you well enough for you to make me unhappy.

(*A pause.*)

KAREN. Is that what we have to look forward to? You getting to know me better, so I can make you unhappy?

(*A pause.*)

ROGER. You could probably answer that better than I could.

(*A silence—THEY gaze at each other. A sexual tension begins to surface.*)

ROGER So what's the problem with you and Bob?
KAREN. Are you just having fun with me?
ROGER. Not yet.
KAREN. (*Chuckling uneasily.*) Well, let's just say Bob has very strong opinions.
ROGER. About what?

(*A pause.*)

KAREN. (*Sighing uncomfortably.*) How I dress. Who my friends are. How I wear my hair.

(*ROGER stares.*)

KAREN. (*A pause.*) You really interested in this?
ROGER. Uh huh, this is our deal. I'll show you mine, if you'll show me yours.

(*A silence—SHE just looks at him.*)

KAREN. My what?
ROGER. Life.

(*MATT sticks his head in the door.*)

MATT. They need you for another lineup.

(*A pause.*)

ROGER. We haven't shot anything yet. What are they lining up now?
MATT. (*Defensively.*) I don't know.
ROGER. (*A look at Karen.*) I'll be right back.

(HE goes. KAREN puts on recorder and begins to dictate.)

KAREN. How does a star gain favor with the press? Astonishingly, after revealing himself an emotional basket case—*(In a more intimate voice—a note to self.)* A little strong—Carstairs suddenly became suggestive, and seemed to turn the most innocent question toward flirtation. *(To self.)* I think ... I decided to see just how far he intended to go. *(A pause.)* Part of me felt flattered, and even a tiny bit attracted ... *(To self.)* Scratch that—Bob would kill. Where would Roger Carstairs' career desperation take him? *(Slowly.)* Given—enough—rope.

(SHE clicks off the tape and sits there a moment, then removes her jacket and unbuttons the bottom button on her dress to reveal more leg. ROGER enters and sees her unbutton the button. HE watches for a moment from the door. KAREN turns suddenly and sees him. She is startled. HE walks C. to get a better look and smiles— then crosses L. to the director's chair and sits.)

ROGER. Where are you from originally?

(A pause.)

KAREN. Cleveland.
ROGER. What were you doing in Cleveland?
KAREN. O.K. I'll give you the short version.
ROGER. Karen ...

(SHE reacts to the first time HE's called her by name and watches him carefully.)

ROGER. Give me the long version. I can handle it.

(*A pause.*)

KAREN. The Ringstads are from Scotland, going back to about the fourteenth century.

ROGER. Who are the Ringstads?

KAREN. That's me. Karen Ringstad. You didn't know my name?

ROGER. (*Unapologetically.*) No.

MATT. (*Knocks.*) I just took a call from Judy. She says she won't be back until late tonight, and she'll come over here and see you tomorrow morning.

ROGER. Why didn't she call me here?

MATT. (*Defensively.*) I don't know. I just took the message.

ROGER. Where is she now?

MATT. She didn't say.

(*A pause.*)

ROGER. This is my son, Matt. This is Karen Ringstad.

MATT. Hi.

KAREN. Hello. You want to be in this profession?

MATT. (*Highly defensive.*) I don't know.

(*There is an uncomfortable silence. MATT turns to leave.*)

MATT Nice to have met you.

KAREN. Nice to have met you.

(*MATT goes. KAREN crosses to ROGER.*)

KAREN. Who's Judy?

(*There is a silence as ROGER considers whether HE wants to talk about this.*)

ROGER. We're not friends. We're just lovers.

KAREN. That's cute. Did you just make that up, or is that an old line?

ROGER. (*Looks at her.*) I just made it up.

KAREN. Very cute. Is she an actress?

ROGER. It's Judith Ivory.

KAREN. Judith Ivey. Oh, she's brilliant.

ROGER. Not Judith Ivey. Judith Ivory.

KAREN. Judith Ivory. Oh, she's very beautiful. She works in TV a lot. Right?

ROGER. Right.

KAREN. (*Crosses back to sofa and sits where all her notes are.*) She's beautiful. How long have you been seeing her?

ROGER. About three months. She's got wonderful qualities. If she gets the right parts, she could be a major actress.

KAREN. You haven't been seen out with her.

ROGER. We stay in bed a lot.

KAREN. You've never talked publicly about a relationship before, have you?

ROGER. (*Rises and crosses to sofa. Smiling.*) I'm hoping it will help hold this one together.

KAREN. Is it shaky? Is that why you're giving her a plug?

ROGER. I wasn't giving her a plug. I was just telling you about her.

KAREN. That's a plug.

(*HE sits on the sofa, close to her.*)

ROGER. I guess so, but I mean it. A lot of times, people say stuff they don't mean.

KAREN. And you don't?

ROGER. No.

KAREN. Never?

ROGER. No. If I say something, I can be trusted. (*A pause.*) And you?

KAREN. You mean, do I lie?

ROGER. Yeah.

KAREN. No.

ROGER. (*Pointedly.*) So, if I asked you a question, I'll definitely get an honest answer.

(*A pause.*)

KAREN. Yeah.

(*HE stares at her in silence.*)

KAREN. Is it a shaky relationship?

ROGER. All relationships can use help, can't they?

(*A pause.*)

KAREN. Why does it need help?

ROGER. Why do you and Bob need help?

KAREN. We're talking about you and Judith now.

ROGER. I'm too involved in my work. I don't put the needed amount of time in a relationship. That's a full-time job, and I don't handle two full-time jobs—great.

KAREN. (*Nods understandingly.*) So how do you solve that?

ROGER. You know the problem?

KAREN. Yeah.

ROGER. You do what you can. You hope it's enough, and if it's not, you try to give more; and if you can't, you get out. You don't steal the other person's time pretending to be someone you're not.

(*A pause.*)

KAREN. What if you're not 100% sure who you are?
ROGER. Then you better 100% try to find out.
KAREN. Do you completely know who you are?
ROGER. (*Looking at her. It's a romantic moment.*) I'm discovering it all the time.
KAREN. Me, too. (*A pause. SHE smiles at him.*) Do you think you'll marry her?
ROGER. Do you think I should talk about that in a magazine?

(*A silence.*)

KAREN. O.K., now *I'd* like to go off the record.
ROGER. (*Teasing her.*) You would?
KAREN. Yeah.

(*ROGER nods.*)

KAREN. Do you think you'll marry her?

(*A pause.*)

ROGER. Why is that so important for you to know?

(*SHE gazes at him. There is a strong sexual tension. SHE watches him closely.*)

ROGER. (*Simply.*) No. I think she's going to come here tomorrow and break up with me.

KAREN. (*Startled.*) Why do you say that?

ROGER. Because I've been through this before. I think she's with someone right now, and that's why she didn't call me here. I deserve it. I haven't been able to give her enough.

KAREN. Could you give anybody enough?

(*THEY stare. The sexual tension builds. Each tries to figure what the other is doing.*)

ROGER What do you want from the man in your life?

KAREN. (*Knows it's provocative.*) I want him to sleep with me.

(*THEY stare at each other. There is a KNOCK at the door, and MARIO bursts in. HE crosses L. to his table.*)

MARIO. Boy, these special effects take forever! They're so complicated. Jay's not talkin' to anybody. He's just lookin' off into space. They can't get it to work right—but I don't even know *what* they can't get to work right. (*Goes to a pack of cigarettes HE had left.*) Here they are. I'm down to seven a day. (*HE crosses to Roger.*) First day I'm makin' up a very, very big superstar, who should remain nameless, Mr. X. I finish, I light up a cigarette. He says, "Hey, I don't like no one smokin' around me." I say, "O.K., Mr. X—no problem." I put it out. A little later— he goes into the bathroom—I hear the toilet flush—he comes out—I go in, I see the sink is dry. I come out. I light up—He says, "Hey, I thought I told you, no smoking." I say, "Mr. X, you urinate—you don't wash your hands—I can have a smoke."

(*ROGER and KAREN laugh.*)

MARIO. We were the best of friends after that! (*A pause.*) Tremendous guy! (*A pause; ruefully.*) But he was a very big star who urinated and didn't wash his hands. It takes all kinds. (*HE crosses U.C. to door.*)

ROGER. (*Beckoning him back. A pause.*) Mario, who's Mr. X?

MARIO. (*HE crosses to Roger.*) Oh no, Roger. It's not right to say.

ROGER. Stays in this room.

MARIO. Not in front of Miss Ringstad.

ROGER. Whisper in my ear.

MARIO. Not to be repeated?

ROGER. I promise.

(*MARIO whispers in Roger's ear.*)

ROGER. (*Teasing.*) Really! Get out of here! No way!

MARIO. (*Raises his right hand.*) Swear to God. (*A pause.*) I mean, c'mon!

(*There is a KNOCK on the door, and PETE, the motor home man enters.*)

PETE. Roger, I can get a low-cal apple juice. You interested?

ROGER. (*Crosses to his director's chair and sits. Teasing.*) You trying to tell me something, Pete?

PETE. Whatya mean?

ROGER. Y'know, with the camera adding ten pounds...

PETE. Oh no, Roger, my God, no!

ROGER. (*Teasing.*) Did someone ask you to slip some low-cal stuff in here?

MARIO. (*Laughing*.) He's kiddin'. He's kiddin' ... Tremendous.

(*MARIO leaves.*)

ROGER. Does it *taste* like apple juice?
PETE. Yeah. Pretty much.
ROGER. (*Still teasing.*) *Pretty* much!?
PETE. (*Going out the door.*) Forget I brought it up. You look great.

(*ROGER and KAREN are alone. HE smiles at her.*)

KAREN. Who's Mr. X?
ROGER. (*Smiling.*) I promised.
KAREN. (*Crosses to C.*) Do you exercise?
ROGER. Some ... yeah.
KAREN. How much?
ROGER. Five minutes.
KAREN. What do you do for five minutes?
ROGER. I have a back thing I do. It also gives you a well-developed chest and shoulder area. (*HE crosses to her.*) Want to see it?
KAREN. What?
ROGER. My chest and shoulder area.
KAREN. (*Chuckling.*) Only if you feel you have to show it to me.

(*HE stares at her. A pause.*)

KAREN. In general, what kind of a woman interests you?
ROGER. An interesting woman.
KAREN. Is Judith interesting?

(*A pause.*)

ROGER. Is Bob interesting?

KAREN. We're talking about you and Judith. (*A pause.*) Why do you want to know if Bob is interesting?

ROGER. (*Stares at her.*) For the same reason you want to know if Judith is interesting.

(*A silence—the sexual tension is there again.*)

ROGER. Why don't you ask me if I'm a breast man, a leg man, or a (*Looks around slightly toward her behind.*) man.

KAREN. Because you'd ask me if I was a chest woman, a leg woman, or a (*Looks around slightly toward his behind.*) woman.

ROGER. Are you?

KAREN. No. Are you?

ROGER. No.

(*A pause.*)

KAREN. You're lying a little.

ROGER. So are you.

(*THEY share a warm chuckle. A silence.*)

KAREN. (*Again trying to get the interview on a comfortable footing. SHE crosses D.R.*) What's the hardest thing about movie-making?

ROGER. (*HE crosses D.C.*) Sitting and waiting, like I'd be if you weren't here—So, I'm glad you're here even though I don't trust you.

KAREN. You don't trust me?

ROGER. No.

KAREN. Why?

(*A pause.*)

ROGER. I think this piece is going to attack me.

(*A pause.*)

KAREN. (*Uncomfortable.*) Why do you think that?
ROGER. I went to show Cappy the ad and saw your notes by mistake.

(*A pause.*)

KAREN. What did they say?
ROGER. "Egotistical. Self-centered. Look for narcissism."
KAREN. (*Crosses to him.*) Those are notes for questions.
ROGER. (*Stares at her.*) You're lying. You said you wouldn't lie, but you're lying.

(*A tense silence.*)

KAREN. Why would I want to attack you?
ROGER. You don't. You were assigned to.
KAREN. Why do you say that?
ROGER. Because that's how it works. It's Bob's idea, I bet. Women usually like me—certain kinds of men don't...
KAREN. What kind of men?—
ROGER. (*Pointedly.*) Tight-ass men. A hatchet job is emotional rape. (*A pause.*) You're uncomfortable. That's a good sign.
KAREN. A sign of what?

ROGER. That you're capable of being embarrassed—and ...

KAREN. What?

ROGER. That you have feeling for me—like I do for you—

(*KAREN stares at him.*)

ROGER. That I haven't just imagined what's been going on here.

(*A pause.*)

KAREN. (*Softly.*) What's been going on here?

(*HE takes her into his arms and kisses her. A long silence.*)

KAREN   It's these motor homes ... It all seems unreal...

(*HE is gazing at her face.*)

KAREN. You're so quiet ...

ROGER. I'm memorizing.

KAREN. You don't have to memorize—just do it ...

ROGER. (*HE kisses her deeply.*) Want a drink? (*HE crosses to refrigerator and takes out a bottle of wine.*)

KAREN. It's morning! (*Silence; amazed.*) I've known you for an hour. (*A silence.*) Will you have a drink?

ROGER. I can't while I'm working. I will later. (*HE pours her some wine.*)

KAREN. (*Crosses U.C.*) Later? Is there going to be a later?

(*HE stares at her and nods. A long pause.*)

KAREN I need to ask you something. (*A pause.*) Are you doing this, because you expect this to be a good piece?

ROGER. (*Meaning sex.*) I certainly hope so.

KAREN. I'm talking about the interview.

ROGER. You think I'm thinking about the interview?

(*A silence.*)

KAREN. (*Stares at him.*) Well ... You are romantic. (*A pause.*) I'm sorry, I'm nervous.

ROGER. Me too.

KAREN. Really? Honestly?

ROGER. (*Crosses past her.*) Yeah.

KAREN. What are you nervous about?

ROGER. I'm afraid at some point you're going to reject me.

KAREN. Would that be a good idea?

ROGER. That would be a terrible idea.

KAREN. That's what I think.

ROGER. (*Crosses to her.*) You do?

(*SHE nods. HE kisses her again.*)

KAREN. (*Struggling with herself.*) We're both involved ...

ROGER. I'm not. She's going to leave me tomorrow.

KAREN. You seriously believe that?

ROGER. Uh huh.

KAREN. So this is pre-rebound.

(*There is a KNOCK on the door. ROGER moves quickly away from Karen—just as MATT sticks his head in.*)

MATT. Jay said to say he's *really* sorry, but he's drowning in special effects, and he can already see he's not going to get to you today.

(*ROGER stares a long moment—then nods. MATT goes. ROGER walks to the door and locks it. HE then pours himself a glass of wine.*)

ROGER. I knew this was going to happen as soon as I met you.
KAREN. You did?
ROGER. In a couple of minutes. There was a certain possibility about you. And I knew I was ... a possibility.
KAREN. Before you knew Judith was going to leave you?
ROGER. That was just a question of time.
KAREN. And you knew this was going to happen?
ROGER. I knew this *could* happen.
KAREN. What *is* this?
ROGER. What *is* this? That's the best question you've asked all day.

(*HE walks to the bedroom door, turns and looks at her. SHE hesitates then walks toward him, turns back to pick up her glass of wine and walks slowly toward him. HE takes her hand. THEY walk into the bedroom and kiss.*)

CURTAIN

ACT II

AT RISE: It's the following morning. ROGER is alone in the motor home, on the phone.

ROGER. (*Pacing.*) Uh huh ... Uh huh ... Right. Yeah ... So that's like three people are in the theatre watching the first show ... How much *is* a senior citizen's? So maybe we have five people ... You got any figures from Chicago? What do you mean, nothing? Literally, nothing? You mean nobody's in the theatre? You sure they have a 12:00 show? No, I know it's early. You can't really tell until we get the weekend ... Doug, do me a favor. Call that theatre in Chicago just to make sure someone remembered to unlock the doors, 'cause *that* could really slow things down ... Let me know if you hear anything you think I'd like to hear. Thanks, Doug. Bye. (*HE punches in a number.*) *Vanity Fair* Magazine, please. (*Punches in the number.*) Karen Ringstad, please. Uh ... Just say, uh, Roger called. Thanks. (*HE goes to door, opens it and looks out.*) Pete! Would you check the stage if any messages came for me, and, uh ... leave a drive-on for Judith Ivory.

PETE. O.K., Roger.

ROGER. Thanks. Let me know.

MARIO. (*From outside, sees Roger and calls to him.*) Roger! Y'know what I want to do? Come over here and sit down. (*MARIO enters and crosses D.L.*) I want to put a little more white liner on the inside of the lid—to bring the eye out a little bit more.

(*ROGER crosses and sits in director's chair.*)

ROGER. (*Teasing.*) Both eyes or one eye?

MARIO. Both eyes. (*A pause.*) "Both eyes or one eye?"! You're kiddin' me! Tremendous!

(*HE laughs. A pause. PETE KNOCKS, opens the door and sticks his head in. MARIO works on Roger.*)

PETE. No messages for you. I left a drive-on for Miss Ivory.

ROGER. Thanks, Pete. Uh ... she didn't need one yesterday, but leave one for Miss Ringstad, too.

PETE. Got it.

ROGER. Thanks.

PETE. You're welcome. (*HE goes.*)

MARIO. How you doin' today, Roger? You seem a little quiet.

ROGER. I'm O.K., Mario, I'm just, uh ...(*Can't begin to put it into words. A pause.*)

MARIO. Years ago—I was making up Mr. Robert Taylor—Quietest man I ever met. I'd say, "Mr. Taylor, how ya doin' this mornin'?" He'd nod for a while—then say, "O.K." I'd say, "Did ya have a nice weekend?" He'd nod for a while—then say, "Uh huh." I'd say, "Can I get you anything?" He'd think for a long time—then just shake his head "no." But that man never had a bad word to say about anyone. He never had a *word* to say about anyone— Fantastic guy!

(*There's a KNOCK on the door.*)

ROGER. C'mon in.

(*CAPPY enters, looking agitated. HE crosses D.R.*)

ROGER. Your cat died?

CAPPY. Something like that.

ROGER. What?

CAPPY. The studio doesn't like "Be be be."

ROGER. After a month's shooting?!

CAPPY. Kraven just got back from Europe, heard it for the first time, and wants me to do something else.

ROGER. Instead of "Be be be"?

CAPPY. Yeah. How does it sound to you?

ROGER. Great!

CAPPY. (*Agitated.*) So what do they want?! You do it. Let me hear it.

ROGER. (*Using creature's voice.*) "Be be be be be."

CAPPY. I love that!

MARIO. Yes.

CAPPY. Kraven heard "Pee pee pee pee."

MARIO. No ...

CAPPY. (*Crosses to C.*) He thinks it sounds like the creature wants to use the bathroom. Where's the logic? Like he uses bathrooms in outer space.

MARIO. (*Trying to be supportive.*) I don't even *believe* in outer space!

(*CAPPY and ROGER look at him.*)

ROGER. (*Trying to be helpful; easily.*) So you'll do something else.

CAPPY. (*Agitated. Pacing.*) What?! This is my character's sound. I hate this goddamned business! Sometimes I want to forget the whole thing—what am I after so much money for? I've got everything I want! Really! I like to fish more than just about anything. I got a cabin. I got a boat.

ROGER. You can give them whatever they want.

CAPPY. (*Upset.*) Yeah, I can give them whatever they want, but it won't be my guy. My guy is (*Creature's*

voice.) "Be be be be be." (*Own voice.*) That's "Be," not
"Pee." Pee sounds like—(*Creature's voice.*) "Pee pee pee
pee pee." (*Own voice.*) Kraven drinks so much, he's got
pee on the brain. (*Heading out the door.*) I don't know who
the hell I am anymore! (*CAPPY is gone.*)

MARIO. (*Shaking his head.*) Terrible.

(*The phone rings. ROGER crosses D.R. and sits on sofa
where the phone is.*)

MARIO. (*Heading out the door.*) O.K., Roger, you're
all set. I'll check with you later.

(*HE goes. ROGER answers the phone as MATT enters.*)

MARIO. (*To Matt.*) Smile!
ROGER. (*On phone.*) Hello. Yeah. Uh huh. O.K.
Good. Thanks. (*HE hangs up; to Matt.*) An exit survey in
New York shows the horse is a *positive* factor not
negative. What did they ask, five people? Three said they
liked it, two said, "enh."

MATT. I want to quit the picture.
ROGER. Why?
MATT. It's boring. I'm a messenger. I'm a go-fer.
ROGER. You're just starting.
MATT. I hate it! Did you hate it when you started?
ROGER. I loved it.
MATT. (*Crosses D.L.*) I work sixteen hours a day and
for what? I don't even get paid.
ROGER. You get paid.
MATT. C'mon! I'm working eighty hours a week, and I
can't even live on my salary. I hate it. Everybody's running
around like we're saving mankind here. It's just another
bullshit movie. Who cares?!

ROGER. A lot of people will be entertained by this movie. People all over the world.

MATT. I hope so, for your sake, but I don't believe it.

ROGER. You never said this before. Why don't you like the movie?

MATT. It's old hat. There's a creature running around, "Pee pee pee."

ROGER. That's "Be be be."

MATT. No, it's not, Dad. The guy's running around trying to get everybody to take a leak.

ROGER. They're fixing that. What else don't you like?

MATT. (*HE crosses to C. Exploding.*) Goddammit! You're more interested in the movie than you are in me!

ROGER. No, I'm not.

MATT. Yes, you are! You and your goddamned career! I'm sick of it! (*As though on phone.*) Is the horse in the ad?! Is the horse not in the ad?! Screw the horse! Screw the ad! Screw the movie! (*HE crosses D.C.*)

ROGER. (*Simply.*) And screw me?

MATT. I didn't say that.

ROGER. But you feel it.

(*A pause.*)

MATT. Yeah, I do.

ROGER. So what do you want to do?

MATT. I don't know. I'm twenty years old. Get off my back! (*HE sits in the easy chair. A pause.*)

ROGER. What will you do tomorrow morning when you get up?

MATT. (*Screaming.*) I don't know! I don't know!

ROGER. How long are you going to keep doing this?

MATT. Doing what?

ROGER. Beating me up ...

MATT. Beating *you* up?!

ROGER. You're still beating me up, because I wasn't around enough when you were little.

MATT. Who's talking about when I was little?!

ROGER. That's what you're always talking about.

MATT. You've had too much therapy!

ROGER. You haven't had enough.

MATT. I'm still young.

(*The PHONE rings. ROGER answers, crosses behind Matt and pushes down hard on his shoulders—fooling around.*)

ROGER. (*On phone.*) Yeah. Uh huh, uh huh. How many theatres? (*A pause. Looks at Matt, self-consciously.*) The horse wasn't in the ad there, was it?

(*MATT snorts and buries his head in his hands. ROGER sits in director's chair.*)

ROGER. Uh huh. O.K. Thanks. (*HE hangs up phone.*)

MATT. How's it doin'?

ROGER. Not too hot.

MATT. I'm sorry.

ROGER. (*A pause; lightly.*) I'm still in the game. (*A pause.*) Look, you want to quit the picture. Quit. You want to get up tomorrow morning and *then* decide what you're going to do—do that. You want to *not* get up tomorrow morning—do that. It'll all come to you when it comes to you.

MATT. What if it never comes to me?

ROGER. I'm interested in you being happy—period. I don't care if you're never rich and famous.

MATT. Really?

ROGER. Do you care if I am?

MATT. No.

ROGER. I'm the same toward you.
MATT. O.K. (*MATT rises.*)
ROGER. Tell Eddie you're leaving. O.K.?
MATT. O.K. (*HE nods—heads toward door.*)
ROGER. Have you spoken to your mother?
MATT. Yeah, I just called her.

(*THEY stare at each other a moment. MATT exits. ROGER crosses and sits in easy chair. PETE enters carrying some paper towels and yogurt. A pause. ROGER reaching out in his loneliness.*)

ROGER. Pete?
PETE. (*Crosses to Roger.*) Excuse me, Roger?
ROGER. What's going on in *your* life?
PETE. Not that much, Roger.

(*A pause.*)

ROGER. How's your Mom?
PETE. She's fine. She loves the photograph. She always asks about you. (*A pause.*) You need anything, Roger?

(*ROGER stares.*)

PETE. Some different kinds of juices?
ROGER. No. Thanks, Pete.
PETE. (*Crosses U.C., then crosses back to Roger.*) *Anything* you need Roger?
ROGER. Just a hit movie, Pete.

(*A pause.*)

PETE. God bless you, Roger.

(*HE exits. There is a KNOCK at the door.*)

ROGER. (*Staring out front.*) C'mon in.

(*BOB enters, 40's, attractive, extremely serious. Intense. BOB is aggressive throughout the scene.*)

BOB. Hi, I'm Bob Lillkins, I'm Karen Ringstad's editor at *Vanity Fair*.

ROGER. (*Rises quickly, goes U.C. to Bob. Trying to conceal his discomfort.*) Hi.

(*THEY shake hands.*)

BOB. I was looking for Karen. I was on the lot, and thought she'd be here.
ROGER. No, I haven't seen her today.
BOB. You expect her, right?
ROGER. Uh ... yeah.
BOB. How's the interview going?
ROGER. Fine.

(*A pause.*)

BOB. (*An edge.*) Good. You have a picture opening today—don't you?
ROGER. Yeah.
BOB. Is it good?

(*A pause.*)

ROGER. *I* like it.

(*A pause.*)

BOB. Well, when Karen shows up, will you tell her to call the office?
ROGER. Yeah.

(*BOB turns to leave.*)

ROGER. Excuse me. You look familiar. Have we met?

(*A pause.*)

BOB. No, not exactly.

ROGER. What do you mean?

(*A pause.*)

BOB. We had a mutual friend.
ROGER. Who's that?
BOB. Eleanor Kellerman.

(*A long pause.*)

ROGER. (*Looks uneasy. ROGER crosses D.L. leans on director's chair.*) Oh ...

BOB. (*Crosses D.C. An edge.*) How *is* Eleanor   Are you in touch?
ROGER. No.
BOB. When was the last time you spoke to her?
ROGER. (*Sits uneasily on edge of director's chair.*) Six years.
BOB. How was she?

ROGER. Fine. She's got a television production company. Produces industrial films ...

BOB. (*Interrupting curtly. Tense.*) Yeah, I know. Good. That's good.

(*A long silence.*)

ROGER. And you?
BOB. What?
ROGER. How are you doing?
BOB. What do you mean?
ROGER. In your life? In your work?

(*A pause.*)

BOB. (*Extremely edgy.*) Fine. I'm fine.

(*An uneasy silence. A duel.*)

BOB. How are you doing in *your* life and work?
ROGER. What's the use of complaining?
BOB. You don't believe in complaining?
ROGER. No.
BOB. (*Aggressively.*) It's only human, don't you think?
ROGER. Yeah. I just don't believe in it.
BOB. You mean, you acknowledge it as human behavior—you just don't do it.
ROGER. Oh, I do it. I'd rather *not* do it. (*A pause.*) I don't like it.

(*A pause.*)

BOB. (*Confrontational.*) Was I complaining about something?
ROGER. I sense a complaint here—yeah, Bob.

(*BOB crosses behind Roger. ROGER crosses to C. A tense silence.*)

ROGER. Eleanor and I were together *after* you and she were.

BOB. A *day* after.

(*A pause.*)

ROGER. I didn't know that.

BOB. She came and told me what happened—after she met you—felt she and I shouldn't see each other anymore—under the circumstances. (*A pause.*) I agreed.

ROGER. It was a surprise?

BOB. A *big* surprise.

ROGER. You thought your relationship was reasonably solid?

BOB. Very—I thought. (*A pause.*) You didn't know that?

ROGER. No.

BOB. (*Crosses to C. Controlling self.*) You knew she was living with me.

ROGER. She told me she was in the process of moving out.

BOB. (*Angry and astonished.*) She actually said to you she was in the process of moving out?

ROGER. I don't honestly remember exactly. I think so.

BOB. I wish she'd have told me. (*A pause.*) Did she leave you, too?

ROGER. (*Ruefully.*) We didn't have much of a relationship left when she met someone. Yeah.

BOB. How long were you with her?

ROGER. Three years. You?

BOB. You don't know?

(*ROGER nods "no."*)

BOB   (*Matter-of-fact.*) Seven years. I thought we'd get married. (*A pause.*) Well ... I gotta get going. If you hear from Karen—tell her to call me.

(*ROGER nods and then turns away uncomfortably. A pause.*)

BOB   Well ... nice to have met you.
ROGER. Nice to have met you. (*A pause. ROGER crosses U.C.—then stops.*)
BOB. I was devastated when this happened. I was in clinical depression for a year. My voice never rose above a monotone—when I was talking at all. (*HE crosses D.C. Shakes his head ruefully.*) You know, when the woman you love leaves you for another man—that man can take on mythic qualities. Seeing you now has demystified a lot of things. I'm not sure what. I can tell you this. I'm glad we're doing a piece on you. (*A pause.*) Well ... see you. (*BOB leaves.*)

(*ROGER walks tiredly over to the easy chair and sits. There is a KNOCK on the door.*)

ROGER   Come in.

(*EVELYN enters quickly and crosses to Roger.*)

EVELYN. He quit the picture.
ROGER. I know. That's O.K. He'll find his way.
EVELYN. He was very upset. I don't blame him. I thought he was fabulous and I heard a "B," not a "P." (*SHE does creature's voice.*) "Be be be be be."

ROGER. *Cappy* quit the picture?!

EVELYN. I went to talk to Jay about "Let it call to you, at least," but he was having a big fight with Cappy. Jay said lately he'd heard "Pe pe," not "Be be," but never mentioned it, since everyone had seemed so pleased. Cappy just left. He said he was going fishing. He said—I love this—he said he didn't know who the creature was anymore. Very upsetting. (*SHE sits on sofa. A silence.*) Want to run it?

ROGER. O.K.

EVELYN. "You can't go—I'm afraid."

ROGER. "Look. There's something there."

EVELYN. "Mark, I'm afraid. Don't do it. Let it call to you, at least."

ROGER. (*Flat.*) "Doris, there's something there. I'm not afraid, I'm excited. Sometimes we don't know what's out there but we go anyway because not to would feel worse. After all, it's not every day a creature from another world shows up in your back yard. Of course, if it turns out to be too tough, I'll be back before the screen door closes."

EVELYN. I love that.

ROGER. (*Simply.*) I'll probably win the Academy Award.

(*There's a KNOCK on the door and MATT sticks his head in.*)

MATT. (*To Evelyn.*) Miss Dunbar, they need you on the set.

EVELYN. (*Nervously.*) What am I doing now?

MATT. I don't know.

EVELYN. (*As SHE heads out the door.*) I'll be back.

ROGER. O.K.

(*EVELYN goes.*)

MATT. (*Crosses D.L. Shyly.*) I'm finishing out the day.
ROGER. Good.
MATT. (*Sarcastically.*) Good.

(*MATT just stands there and looks at Roger.*)

ROGER. You'll be alright. I'm not worrying about you.
MATT. (*Ingenuously.*) Really?
ROGER. Really.
MATT. (*Leaving.*) I'll talk to you later.
ROGER. O.K.

(*As MATT leaves, MARIO enters and sits on sofa.*)

MARIO. Boy, is it slow out there. They're reshootin' somethin' we shot two weeks ago. (*MARIO crosses to makeup table.*) I wonder if you'll work today. Eddie Quinlan says it's like the old joke ...

(*There's a KNOCK on the door.*)

ROGER. C'mon in.

(*KAREN enters. SHE has a new hair style.*)

MARIO. Eddie Quinlan says it's like the old joke. Oh, hello Miss Ringstad, how are you?

(*ROGER swings around—longingly needing to see her. THEY stare at each other.*)

KAREN. Fine. How are you? (*SHE smiles at Roger. KAREN crosses D.R.—sits on sofa.*)

MARIO. Boy is it slow out there. Eddie Quinlan says it's like the old joke. (*Crosses to C.*) These two guys open up a clothes store. The first day they sell a suit. The second day, they don't sell anything. One guy says to the other guy, "Don't worry, it can't get any worse than this." The third day, the guy that bought the suit the first day brings it back. Incredible! (*To Karen, by way of explanation.*) We're reshooting stuff we shot two weeks ago.

(*KAREN nods.*)

MARIO. (*To Roger.*) You might not work today. (*Looking at Roger.*) Wait a minute. Let me see something. Come over here. (*MARIO crosses D.R. to his makeup kit.*)

ROGER. (*Puts his hands over his face.*) Mario!

MARIO. Get over here. Sit!

(*ROGER goes to the makeup chair as MARIO fusses over a makeup change.*)

MARIO. I hear Mr. Coleman isn't with us anymore—

ROGER. Cappy quit the picture. They didn't like "Be be be". (*To Karen.*) Nat Kraven, the head of production, just got back from Europe—heard it for the first time, and thought it sounded like "Pe pe pe."

(*KAREN smiles.*)

MARIO. These executives ... That's terrible. O.K. Roger, you're all set. I'll see you on the stage. "Be be be" ... I love that. I don't know anymore. (*MARIO goes.*)

*(ROGER and KAREN cross to C. HE takes Karen in his
arms, and kisses her fully.)*

KAREN. Hi.

ROGER. How'd you sleep?

KAREN. I slept great, until I woke up in the middle of
the night and remembered what happened. *(A pause.)* How
are you?

ROGER. The picture's opening soft.

KAREN. With the horse in the ad?

ROGER. With and without the horse.

KAREN. You can tell already?

ROGER. You get an indication from the first couple of
shows. I think people will like it when they see it—so
maybe they'll tell other people, and it will pick up.

KAREN. That happens—right?

ROGER. *(Kidding.) Once,* in 1947. No, it happens. We
won't really know anything till after the weekend, so I'm
going to try to forget it till then.

KAREN. Know what I did after I got my hair done?

ROGER. What? Oh, you got your hair done! I love it!

KAREN. *(SHE smiles.)* After I got my hair done, I
went to see the picture.

ROGER. Really? *(ROGER is touched.)*

KAREN I loved it. I thought you were great!

ROGER. As good as the horse?

KAREN. Well ... the horse is pretty damned good ...

ROGER. How many people were there in the theatre?

KAREN. Oh, it was the first show.

ROGER. You weren't the only one there, were you?

KAREN. Of course not, there were some people.

ROGER. *(Sardonically.)* But you could get a seat.

KAREN *(Smiles.)* You were wonderful, darling.

ROGER. *(Kisses her on the cheek.)* Thanks.

KAREN. I didn't want to come by earlier, because I knew Judith was coming. What happened?

(*ROGER crosses away and stands by director's chair.*)

ROGER. She didn't show up, but Bob did.
KAREN. Bob?!
ROGER. He was on the lot, said he was looking for you.
KAREN. Really?
ROGER. I found out why he sent you to do a slam on me.
KAREN. (*Crosses to him.*) Why?
ROGER. (*Starts to speak, then turns away, then turns back to her. Uncomfortably.*) It seems that Bob and I once knew the same woman, and he feels I took her away from him.
KAREN. Are you kidding?
ROGER. No.
KAREN. Who?!
ROGER. Her name is Eleanor Kellerman.
KAREN. When was this?
ROGER. He's never mentioned her name?
KAREN. No.

(*ROGER shakes his head ruefully.*)

KAREN. What happened?
ROGER. She was seeing him—I met her—then she was seeing me. He said it devastated him. (*A pause.*) He said he'd thought they'd get married.
KAREN. (*Amazed.*) Eleanor Kellerman. Wait. That was the woman in the restaurant with you when you had that fight.

(*ROGER nods.*)

    KAREN. How long ago was this?
    ROGER. Ten years.
    KAREN. What happened with you and her?
    ROGER. We broke up after about three years.
    KAREN. Why?
    ROGER. Why does anyone break up? (*A pause.*) They get to know the other person.

(*A pause.*)

    ROGER What are you going to tell Bob?
    KAREN. I don't know, Roger. What *should* I tell Bob?

(*A silence—THEY stare at each other. The PHONE rings. ROGER crosses R. to sofa and picks it up.*)

    ROGER. Hello. Hi! I got a message you were going to get in late last night and come by this morning. Uh huh. Uh huh.

(*KAREN is uneasy listening to this. SHE makes a sign to Roger if he wants her to step out. HE shakes his head "no."*)

    ROGER. The picture's opening soft. I only have figures for a few cities. Well, you don't have to stand in line. They put the horse in the ad in New York. A mistake. It's O.K. We really won't know anything until after the weekend, so I'm going to try to not think about it till then. How's Palm Springs? Are you having a good time? Uh huh. Who's all there? Uh huh. Oh, give my love. Uh huh. Who's that? (*ROGER sits on sofa.*) No, I don't know him. What's he do? Uh huh. Well, look ... if you're having such a good time—stay there. Absolutely. Enjoy yourself. I'm fine. Really. No hurry. I've got my hands full here with everything. Yeah—a lot's goin' on—I'll tell you when you get back. O.K.? O.K., what? Oh, go with them—go, go ahead—have a good time. I'll talk to you later. Have a good time. Bye. (*HE hangs up.*) She's having a good time. She's with a group of people I know, all except for one guy, Alan Cosman, a real sweet producer—that's how she referred to him—(*A pause.*) I deserve it. I really didn't pay enough attention to her. So now we have a real sweet producer—that's fair. (*A pause.*) Alan Cosman.

(*A pause.*)

    KAREN. You O.K.?
    ROGER. It never feels good, even if you want it to happen.
    KAREN. Did you want it to happen?
    ROGER. Yes.

(*A pause—HE looks at her.*
KAREN crosses to sofa and sits beside him.)

    ROGER. I really *do* love your hair. I didn't say anything when you came in because I thought you were just combing it different. I can't tell, really, it was "done"—so I guess that's good—right? But I love it, and ...
    KAREN. Roger ... (*THEY kiss.*)
    ROGER. What will you tell Bob?
    KAREN. Is that what you are most interested in?
    ROGER. (*Attempt at lightness.*) The guy already wants to kill me for taking *one* woman from him. (*There is a KNOCK on the door. ROGER moves away from Karen on sofa.*) Come in.

(*CAPPY enters and crosses D.C.*)

ROGER. I heard you walked.
CAPPY. We're talking. If we can agree on a sound, I'll stay.
ROGER. Good.

(*MARIO enters and goes D.L.*)

CAPPY. (*To Karen.*) I've got a few I've been fooling with. But I wanted to run them by you first. I think I'm too in love with "Be be be" to like anything. Try to be objective. (*To Karen.*) You too. Ready?

(*ROGER nods.*)

CAPPY "Reva reva reva reva."
ROGER. (*Kindly.*) It's like a frog calling for his girlfriend, Reva.
MARIO. (*Crosses to behind sofa.*) A frog calling for his girlfriend, Reva. Tremendous! (*Looks at Cappy.*) No offense.
ROGER. (*To Cappy.*) What else?
CAPPY. "Whom whom whom."
ROGER. An owl.
KAREN. An owl.
MARIO. An owl.
CAPPY. It's not "who", it's "whom".
ROGER. Too close.
CAPPY. What if I hit the "M" more? "Who*m* who*m* who*m* who*m*." (*Getting agitated.*) "Who*m*! Who*m*! Who*m*! Who*m*! Who*m*! Who*m*!" I can't do this. The "Be be be" is great It's otherworldly, and it's got a hidden message telling people to be. *Be* who you are. *Be*. It's great! (*In disgust.*) Agh!

ROGER. (*Reluctantly.*) It *is* great. Got anything else?

CAPPY. One more. But it's no good either.

ROGER. Let me hear it!

CAPPY. (*Dismissively.*) "*M*wah *m*wah *m*wah."

ROGER. Do it again.

CAPPY. "*M*wah *m*wah *m*wah."

ROGER. (*Grudgingly, thoughtfully.*) I like that.

CAPPY. Really?!

MARIO. It's like a sound in the wind. Remember that song, "They Call the Wind Mariah."

CAPPY. This is "*M*wah *m*wah *m*wah!"

MARIO. Yeah.

ROGER. Try it as one syllable.

CAPPY. "Mwah mwah mwah"?

ROGER. Yes.

CAPPY. (*Excited.*) "Mwah mwah mwah."

ROGER. Yes.

CAPPY. "Mwah mwah mwah."

ROGER. Calmer.

CAPPY. "Mwah mwah mwah."

ROGER. Softer.

CAPPY. "Mwah mwah mwah."

ROGER. Softer.

CAPPY. Softer?

ROGER. Softer.

CAPPY. (*Very calm.*) "Mwah mwah mwah."

ROGER. I like that.

KAREN. Really.

MARIO. Wonderful.

CAPPY. "Mwah mwah mwah."

ROGER.	KAREN.	MARIO.
Wonderful.	Great.	Excellent.

CAPPY. (*Very happy.*) Maybe you're right. I'm going to do it for Kraven. Thanks. (*As HE goes—excitedly.*) "Mwah! Mwah!"

ROGER. Softer.
CAPPY. (*Calmer.*) "Mwah mwah mwah."
ROGER. That's great. Good for you.

(*CAPPY exits.*)

ROGER. Show business.

(*KAREN laughs.*)

MARIO. I love it. (*Exits.*)
KAREN. That was nice.

(*ROGER crosses U.L.*)

ROGER. So what will you tell Bob?

(*A silence.*)

KAREN. (*Getting edgy.*) What would you like me to tell him?

(*A pause. ROGER is pacing.*)

ROGER. You *don't* live with him?
KAREN. No.
ROGER. And he thinks you're getting married.
KAREN. Occasionally.
ROGER. What have you said about that?
KAREN. About what?
ROGER. About getting married?

(*A pause. SHE goes to him.*)

KAREN. Roger, help me with this. (*A pause.*) You think we could beat the three years you spent with Eleanor Kellerman? I'm a very serious person, Roger. And I think you are too.

ROGER. What's that mean?

(*KAREN sits on the arm of the easy chair C.*)

KAREN. I don't look at last night as a one-night thing, and I don't think you do either.

ROGER. (*Shakes his head "no." A pause.*) It's funny. Then I saw your notes, I was trying to get even with you, trying to make you uncomfortable—

KAREN. And I thought I was getting a good story.

ROGER. (*HE embraces her. Meaning sex came into the air.*) And then at some point ...

KAREN. (*Agreeing.*) At some point ... So sex—is that all this is?

(*A pause.*)

ROGER. (*HE stares at her.*) It's certainly a component.

KAREN. How big a component?

(*THEY kiss. The PHONE rings. ROGER crosses to sofa and picks it up.*)

ROGER. (*HE slowly sits.*) Yeah. (*HE just listens, looking forlorn.*) He called to say that? Thanks. (*HE hangs up and just sits there. A long pause.*)

KAREN. What is it?

ROGER. The guy I'm friends with at the movie company in New York heard from his boss out here, Al Minton. Al Minton says they've gotten terrible figures from all over the country and they've already decided to cut way back on their ads for next week.

(*A pause.*)

KAREN. I'm sorry.

ROGER. (*Sighs.*) They're just being realistic. The advertising is very expensive and they've gotten terrible figures.

KAREN. Gee, I really enjoyed it. They'll pull out of a movie that quickly?

ROGER. (*Nodding.*) They're just being realistic. (*A pause.*) There's a cutoff point here somewhere.

KAREN. What do you mean?

ROGER. (*Takes off his shoes and lies on sofa. Easily.*) Well, at some point they just don't want you anymore. You asked how I felt about *this* movie. This was the only picture that was offered to me in the last year. I'm sure I was about the eighth choice.

KAREN. Oh, c'mon! (*KAREN crosses behind him and sits on arm of sofa and pats him.*)

ROGER. Maybe tenth. (*With humor.*) It used to be me in a movie. Then me and a woman star. Then after a while it was me and a horse. Then me and a creature from outer space. What's next? Me and an insect? Then an insect and me. (*A pause. Joking.*) There's some talk about an ant movie. The red ants attack the black ants. I play the ant keeper who has a nervous breakdown. (*Lightly.*) I'm still in the game.

KAREN. Well, like you said—this one could be very good.

ROGER. That's what I said about the horse.

KAREN. And it is! Why don't you call that guy's boss and see just what those figures are. It's very early for all this negativity ... (*SHE tries to hand him the phone from where she's sitting.*)

ROGER. Oh no. No. That's a call ... I really don't want to make. "Al Minton, please. Hi Al, howya doing?" Oh no! You get sympathy that really doesn't conceal a hatred kind of thing. (*A pause.*) I'll wait till Monday. If there are any good signs maybe I'll call then. In the meantime, I'd love to talk about anything but movies, ads, horses, you, me, Bob.

KAREN. Judith.

ROGER. Alan Cosman.

(*A pause. There is a KNOCK on the door. EVELYN enters. ROGER comes up on one elbow as EVELYN sits on sofa.*)

EVELYN. I talked to Jay about, "Let it call to you at least," and he said, "Cut it." Every time I ask him about anything—he says, "Cut it." If I asked him about everything on my mind—I'd be out of the movie. (*To Karen.*) This is off the record. O.K.

KAREN. Of course.

EVELYN. I think he hates me in the part.

ROGER. He loves you in the part.

EVELYN. What?

ROGER. He loves you in the part.

EVELYN. He said he loves me in the part?

ROGER. Yes.

EVELYN. Out of the blue? He just said that?

ROGER. Not out of the blue. We were talking about everything, and he said it. He said it more than once.

EVELYN. Really?

ROGER. He loves you in the part.

EVELYN. I'm shocked.

ROGER. He loves you.

EVELYN. Oh, I really appreciate hearing this. Why didn't you tell me right away?

ROGER. I should have. I thought you were terrific, and I didn't think you were that worried about it.

EVELYN. I can be embarrassingly bad.

ROGER. C'mon ...

EVELYN. Embarrassingly bad.

ROGER. You're great.

EVELYN. More than once he said he liked me?

ROGER. (*HE embraces her and kisses her on the cheek.*) Loved you. He loves you in the part.

EVELYN. Thanks, Roger. I'll let you get back to your interview.

ROGER. He loves you.

EVELYN. Thanks a lot Roger. (*EVELYN exits.*)

(*ROGER puts on his shoes.*)

KAREN. That was sweet. You really helped her.

ROGER. Evelyn's whole identity comes from her work. Cappy's like that too.

KAREN. Are you like that?

ROGER (*Thinks a moment and shrugs.*) Now, journalists—you hear they have no emotion *but* certain journalists have ... a lot of emotion. A lot of emotion.

(*THEY kiss. CAPPY bursts in, ROGER and KAREN separate quickly. CAPPY paces around C.*)

CAPPY. Kraven loved it! He was in a meeting with four people, but I ran in and said, "Mwah! Mwah! Mwah!" He said, "Great!"

ROGER. Good for you!

CAPPY. He loved it! I ran right out! He loved it!

ROGER. That's terrific.

KAREN. Congratulations.

CAPPY. He just loved it. He said, "Great." (*Pause.*) I'm glad that's over. I was starting to have an identity crisis. It's not that easy to run around for months with "Be be be" and the next day I'm "Mwah mwah mwah."—even if everyone loves it. It's not that easy. (*A pause; quietly.*) I miss "be be be."

ROGER. You'll use it again somewhere.

(*A pause.*)

CAPPY. (*Softly.*) No. I'll never use it again. (*A pause.*) But anyway, thanks for all your patience and support and, *hey,* thanks for picking the one he loved! (*As HE goes.*) Keep kissing. "Mwah, mwah, mwah." (*HE exits.*)

KAREN. (*Uneasily.*) He saw us.

ROGER. It's O.K. (*A pause.*) What's the matter?

KAREN. (*Crosses to C.*) I don't know. It's not that easy to be with someone for two years and then suddenly I'm with someone else. It's not that easy. I'm starting to get nervous. What *should* I tell Bob?

ROGER. (*Crosses U.L. With humor.*) I think you should say, "Bob, I couldn't find enough bad stuff about Roger Carstairs so I can't do the hatchet job, but I think I could write a really great article about him and sell it to the *L.A. Times,* because with his new movie bombing he could use it."

KAREN. Don't joke with me, Roger. I'm not confident enough to know that's a joke. That *is* a joke, isn't it?

(*ROGER makes a dismissive gesture.*)

KAREN. Talk to me, Roger. Tell me the truth.

(*A silence—HE looks at her.*)

ROGER. For better or worse?
KAREN. Yes.
ROGER. (*Uncomfortably.*) I have no idea what you should say to Bob. I have no idea what's ultimately going to happen to us. I don't have a great track record. I don't even know if you should leave Bob. I mean, you know a lot about me—not everything—but a lot more than I know about you ... what do *you* think about this? What do you think life is all about?! What do *you* think should happen here?

(*A pause. SHE stares at him.*)

KAREN. I think life is about coming to do a hatchet job and falling for someone instead. I think life is about feeling left out while all your girl friends are getting married. (*SHE sits on arm of chair C.*)
ROGER. All your girl friends are getting married?
KAREN. I think life is about walking away from someone who uses up too much air in the room and, as it turns out—I, too, think life is about making a difference and being interested in things outside of yourself.

(*A pause.*)

ROGER. (*Ironically.*) Another do-gooder. Who would have thought?

(*Faintly, from outside the trailer, we hear CAPPY doing "Mwah, mwah, mwah," which continues through Roger's next speech. ROGER puts his arm around her and looks out front.*)

ROGER. There's something out there. I'm not afraid. I'm excited. (*HE looks at her.*) Sometimes we don't know what's there, and we go anyway...

(*"Mwah mwahs" stop.*)

ROGER. (*To Karen, tenderly.*) Because not to would feel worse. After all, it's not every day that a creature from another world shows up in your back yard.
KAREN. Of course, if it turns out to be too tough, I'll be back before the screen door closes.
ROGER. You took the words out of my mouth.
KAREN. C'mere, I'll put them back.

(*THEY kiss and move into the bedroom, all the while kissing, and lie on the bed.*)

KAREN. What is this?
ROGER. What is this? *This* is the best thing that's happened to me in a long time. This is ... I wish I could sing.

(*THEY kiss. HE begins to unbutton her blouse.*)

KAREN. (*Softly.*) Don't you think you ought to lock that door? This place is like Grand Central.

(*HE moves through the sliding door toward the front door. There is a KNOCK on the door.*)

ROGER. Just a minute.

(*ROGER closes door to bedroom as BOB opens the front door. KAREN is behind the door in the bedroom.*)

BOB. (*Coming in.*) Was that "Come in?"

ROGER. (*Startled.*) That was "Just a minute."

BOB. Sorry.

ROGER. That's O.K.

BOB. I've just been walking around the lot, since I've talked to you, and I think I owe you an apology.

(*ROGER looks toward the bedroom to see if the door is firmly closed.*)

BOB. You didn't do anything to me. I've resented you all these years. I've gone to all your pictures, and I've sat there hating you and them.

ROGER. You're not alone.

BOB. But you haven't done anything to me. Nobody can take somebody away from somebody unless that person wants to go. I've always known that, but meeting you brought it home to me. You're just a guy like I am. No better. No worse. I've decided to really make an effort to let go of all this resentment toward you.

ROGER. (*Extremely uncomfortable. HE crosses to Bob.*) Yeah ... Well, that's good. Because resentment can just eat you up ... You know ... It can just eat you up ... (*A pause.*) Yeah ...

(*A pause. BOB extends his hand and ROGER uncomfortably shakes it.*)

ROGER. Well, Bob, I appreciate your coming over to say that.

(*Moving him toward door. There is a KNOCK on the door and MARIO enters.*)

MARIO. Roger, Miss Ringstad got a message on the stage to call her office. (*HE looks around.*) Oh, did she just leave?

(*BOB looks edgy. MARIO starts to go—looks at Roger's makeup again.*)

MARIO. Wait a minute. Let me see something. Sit down a second.

(*ROGER looks at Bob and crosses L. to makeup chair. BOB stares at Roger and at the bedroom door. KAREN is standing, listening, on the other side.*)

MARIO. (*As HE works.*) So they liked "Mwah mwah mwah." That's wonderful. My cat makes that noise, and he'd work a lot cheaper than Mr. Coleman. (*HE laughs.*) Tremendous! My cat! My cat can make some noises. "Meow meow meow - mwah mwah mwah." My cat never stops talking. What a cat!

(*ROGER is intensely trying to figure out what to do. KAREN in the bedroom is in the same state as Roger. BOB is transfixed, trying to figure out what's going on. HE crosses to Roger and glares at him.*)

MARIO. (*A pause.*) I'm makin' up Mr. Henny Youngman. I said, "Mr. Youngman, I enjoy your one-liners as much as the next guy, but I can't make you up if you keep talkin'." He says, "What's the matter, Mario, you afraid I'm going to eat your sponge?"

(*KAREN quietly opens the bathroom door and flushes the toilet. BOB reacts—still trying to figure it out.*)

MARIO. He's great! He says, "Mario, I want you with me on all my pictures." I said, "Mr. Youngman, you don't *make* pictures."

(*KAREN walks through the door.*)

MARIO. Oh, Miss Ringstad, you got a message to call your office from a Mr. Pill, or something.
KAREN. (*Easily.*) Bob! Hi.

(*BOB just stares at her—then back at Roger.*)

MARIO. I said, "Mr. Youngman—maybe you and me could be a team—I make you laugh, and you make the audience laugh." He said, "I already got enough partners— my wife" —Y'know, "take my wife—*please*"—
BOB. (Exploding.) Shut up!

(*There is a long silence.*)

MARIO. (*Baffled.*) What's wrong? (*To Roger.*) Something wrong?

(*ROGER nods slowly. MARIO looks around, trying to figure out what's going on. HE can't, but finally picks up the tension.*)

MARIO. All right, Roger. I'll check you on the set. (*HE goes.*)

(*A silence. EVERYONE is very tense.*)

BOB. (*Edgily.*) You got your hair done.
KAREN. Yes.

BOB. (*Subtly challenging.*) You didn't mention that you wanted to do that.

KAREN. (*Matter-of-fact.*) No. (*A pause.*) It was a whim.

BOB. (*An edge of disdain.*) A *whim*? (*A pause.*) What are you doing, Karen? What's going on?

KAREN. I was using the bathroom.

BOB. How long have you been here?

KAREN. About fifteen minutes.

(*A pause.*)

BOB. How's it going?

KAREN. Fine.

(*A silence.*)

BOB. (*To Roger.*) Tell me I'm being crazy.

KAREN. (*Starting to shake her head to tell him he's not crazy.*) You're not ...

ROGER. (*Crosses to Bob. Quickly jumping in.*) You *are* crazy, Bob. If you're thinking what I think you're thinking ...

KAREN. Roger.

ROGER. Karen, Bob and I once went out with the same woman, and it turns out he's had a thing about me. Bob, if you think what I think you're thinking.

(*ROGER shakes his head. BOB just stares blankly at Roger.*)

ROGER. (*HE speaks quickly.*) Agenda, Bob. It's on your agenda to be suspicious, just like it's on my agenda to fear danger. Whenever I travelled, I always had to make sure

there were plenty of locks and chains on the doors—I
would lie awake in these hotel rooms at night and say,
"There isn't any danger. There isn't any danger—there isn't
any danger"—and pretty soon I didn't need so many locks
and chains. (*Attempt at humor.*) —Oh, maybe a couple—

(*ROGER chuckles. BOB doesn't respond.*)

ROGER. But not so bad. "There isn't any danger. There
isn't any danger." (*A pause.*) There isn't any danger, is
there, Bob?

(*A long, tense silence.*)

BOB. (*Trying to convince himself.*) You're saying she's
doing an interview, and she's using the bathroom.
ROGER. Exactly. Good for you, Bob. Seriously.
(*ROGER crosses to director's chair and sits.*)

(*BOB stares at Roger.*)

ROGER. Agenda.

(*A long pause.*)

BOB. (*Trying to relax. To Karen.*) It's going all right?
KAREN. Yes.
BOB. How much more time do you think you need?
KAREN. I'm just winding up. I'll probably be back in
the office in an hour.
BOB. Good. Uh ... (*To Roger.*) Sorry about all the ...
sorry ...
ROGER. (*Dismissing the necessity of an apology.*) Oh
please!

BOB. (*Heading for door.*) O.K., see you soon. Bye.

KAREN. Bye.

ROGER. Bye.

(*BOB goes. A pause.*)

KAREN. You lied. (*A pause.*) I was going to tell the truth! I was going to tell him he *wasn't* crazy!

ROGER. *He's* not crazy. *You're* crazy! The guy just decided he didn't hate my guts for something that happened ten years ago, and you want me to tell him ... Are you familiar with the phrase, "justifiable homicide?"

KAREN. But you lied! You said you never lied. That was important.

ROGER. I've never been in a situation like this. What was my choice?! What could I have said? (*HE crosses right. Sardonically.*) "Yes, Bob, you're right, Karen and I have slept together. In fact, we were *just* about to do it again. (*Chuckles.*) Y'know, it's pretty much the same thing that happened with Eleanor. It's funny in a way—don't you think so, Bob? Ha, ha, ha, ha. Why, Bob, why are you looking at me like that? You're not *mad,* are you?" (*To Karen.*) C'mon!

KAREN. You didn't stand up for us. You lied instead of standing up for us. You were worried about how Bob feels rather than how I feel.

ROGER. I was worried about death!

KAREN. You're not really committed to anything but yourself and your career, are you?

(*A pause.*)

ROGER. No more than millions of people.

KAREN. (*A pause.*) I don't think you *were* joking about selling a piece to the *Times* about what a great guy you are.

(*A pause.*)

ROGER. Maybe I wasn't.

KAREN. (*Stares at him.*) And maybe that *is* why you slept with me.

ROGER. No.

KAREN (*Crosses DR.*) This is not unfamiliar to me.

ROGER. What?

KAREN Hearing what I want to hear. (*A pause.*) You *told* me. You're too involved in your work. You said it. "It's a full-time job." You probably didn't commit to your wife—to Eleanor—to Judith ...

ROGER. You mean telling Bob we slept together would be committing ... I couldn't have said that. It would have been inhuman.

KAREN. What if there was no Bob?

ROGER. Then we would have slept together in *half* an hour.

KAREN. (*Crosses to C.*) Don't try to joke your way out of this!

ROGER. (*HE moves toward her.*) Out of what?

KAREN. The truth!

ROGER. What's the truth?

KAREN. You didn't spare Bob to help him, you did it to help yourself. *You* came first, right?

(*A long pause.*)

ROGER. Right.

KAREN. You'll always do what makes *you* feel good. You're self-involved.

ROGER. Please don't lecture me about character! You had sex with me after knowing me an hour. (*A pause. ROGER looks extremely sorry for what he's said. A pause.*)

KAREN. You know how to make all the pretty speeches. "The degree you can have feelings for things outside yourself is your measure as a person." I agree with you. What degree can *you* have feelings for things outside yourself?

(*A long pause. ROGER considers it and looks pained.*)

ROGER. Not enough, I guess.

KAREN. (*Crosses D.R.*) You've got the perfect job. You're a movie star. You're supposed to be a narcissist. You probably wouldn't have gotten to be a movie star if you weren't. (*A pause.*) Maybe if there had been no Bob, I wouldn't have slept with you in half an hour. I wouldn't have slept with you at all. I've become too needy, but this isn't what I need. (*A pause.*) I'm going to go to Bob, tell him what happened, and then I'm going to leave him.

ROGER. (*HE looks at floor.*) And I'm going into the witness protection program.

(*A pause.*)

KAREN. (*Crosses U.C. and picks up her large bag.*) So long, Roger.

ROGER. Oh no!

KAREN. (*Crosses to him. With great difficulty.*) I'm sorry.

(*ROGER looks surprised.*)

KAREN. (*With difficulty.*) I know you think I'm crazy and that I'm overreacting, but I can see the end of this before it really begins and I don't have any more time to waste. I want somebody who can give a whole lot to me and hopefully some day soon a family. And that's not you, Roger. That's just not you. (*A pause.*) There *is* a danger, Roger, but it has nothing to do with locks and chains. There's a danger of leading an empty life. (*SHE leaves.*)

(*ROGER stands there a long moment without moving. HE seems very upset. Then HE slowly goes to the phone. HE sits on sofa—holding a pillow. HE punches in a number on the phone.*)

ROGER. (*In great discomfort; on phone.*) Al Minton, please. (*A pause.*) Roger Carstairs calling. (*A long pause.*) Hi, Al, howya doin'? (*A pause.*) Yeah, they were disappointing, but you really feel you know the weekend from these early figures? (*A pause.*) Uh huh, uh huh, yeah, uh huh, well ... Al, excuse me a second. I know you're discussing next week's ad budget already, and I just want to say I can get a couple days off what I'm shooting here and fly to New York, and get on "Good Morning, America." The producer is a close friend. Or the "Today" show. I have good relationships there. (*A pause.*) I'm talking film clips that maybe five million people would see. We've got great clips, outstanding clips, and ... uh huh, uh huh ... well, let me ask you this, Al—Is there anything at all that I can do to get you to hang in there with me a little bit longer? (*A pause.*) Uh huh. I understand. You know, Al, they put the horse in the ad in New York by mistake! No, I know it didn't make any difference. (*A pause. HE is controlling his upset.*) I understand. I understand. Uh huh. Yeah. Thank *you.* I understand. Thank *you.* Bye.

(*HE hangs up the phone and sits there for a long moment. There is a KNOCK on the door and MATT enters.*)

MATT. Got a minute?
ROGER. Sure.
MATT. (*Looking very uncomfortable.*) I was thinking
...
ROGER. Yeah ... (*HE slowly crosses L. to behind director's chair.*)
MATT. Maybe I'll stay on the movie.
ROGER. Oh yeah?
MATT. (*Shifting his feet uncomfortably.*) Like you say—what am I going to do when I get up tomorrow morning?
ROGER. Do whatever you want to do.
MATT. Maybe I'd want to come here.

(*A pause—ROGER studies him.*)

ROGER. You don't have to do that.
MATT. Maybe I'd want to ...
ROGER. Why? You hate it.

(*A pause.*)

MATT. (*Looking at the floor.*) Maybe I want to be around you.

(*A pause.*)

ROGER. Around me?
MATT. (*Smiling.*) You and your horse in the ad.
ROGER. (*Smiling.*) By next week the ads will be so small there couldn't be a horse.
MATT. (*Ironically.*) So you won.

ROGER. The week after that—there won't be any ad. (*Roger chuckles.*)

MATT. What are you laughing about?

(*A pause.*)

ROGER. Not that *you* need to hear this.

MATT. What?

ROGER. This is for anyone but you.

MATT. What?

ROGER. (*Rueful laugh.*) Be careful how much you give to work—You could end up ... (*ROGER turns away and tries to control his extreme upset. A silence.*)

MATT. We'll be O.K. (*A pause. MATT crosses to sofa and sits beside ROGER.*) I like that new sound—that "Mwah mwah mwah ..."

ROGER. Oh yeah?

MATT. Yeah ... (*A pause.*) Maybe this picture *will* be something.

ROGER. (*With an attempt at humor.*) Well ... it will be something. It will definitely be *something*.

(*A pause.*)

MATT. (*Trying to cheer him up.*) Hey, Dad, you're still in the game.

(*A pause. MARIO bursts in. HE crosses to sofa.*)

MARIO. Roger, wait until you hear this! You're not working today—again! Eddie Quinlan says they can't get the shot of the creature disappearing off into space. They can't get the shot! Something with the special photography—I don't know, the creature just won't disappear. Anyway, you're finished. (*MARIO crosses L. and collects his materials.*) Incredible!

(*A silence.*)

ROGER. (*To Matt.*) Feel like taking a walk?
MATT. Where?
ROGER. (*Shrugs.*) When was the last time you and me took a walk?
MATT. (*Thinks.*) I don't remember *any* walks.

(*A pause.*)

ROGER. (*Rises. HE crosses U.C.*) C'mon, and then maybe we'll get some lunch.

(*MATT crosses U.C. ROGER packs up briefcase. ROGER thinks a moment.*)

ROGER Then maybe later—we'll pop in—catch the movie—see how it plays in front of an audience.

(*A pause.*)

MATT. (*Meaning Roger.*) The creature just won't disappear—(*MATT pats Roger on the back and follows him out the door.*)
MARIO. Tremendous!

CURTAIN

COSTUME PLOT

ROGER
ACT I—burgundy shirt, blue jeans, lt. grey socks, white
    sneakers, ring.
ACT II—blue denim shirt, lt. grey pleated pants, beige
    socks, lt. brown deck shoes, brown belt.

PETE
ACT I—brown plaid shirt, khaki jacket, khaki pants,
    brown belt, grey socks, casual suede oxfords, watch.
ACT II—Plaid shirt, same pants, same accessories.

MATT
ACT I—green polo shirt, grey baggy pants, denim jacket,
    white socks, white sneakers, walkie-talkie.
ACT II—Orange t-shirt, khaki pants, remainder same as
    Act I.

MARIO
ACT I—red/green/beige shirt, grey pleated pants, gold
    makeup jacket, gold necklaces, rings, white sneakers,
    white socks, belt.
ACT II—blue/white stripe shirt, brown pants, gold
    makeup jacket, remainder same as Act I.

KAREN
ACT I—lt.blue sleeveless silk top w/matching skirt, white
    linen jacket, grey lizard belt, hoop earrings, watch, off-
    white sling back open toe pumps. Remove: jacket
    onstage
ACT II—beige silk short-sleeve blouse, pink/grey flower
    (silk) print skirt, rose cotton cardigan sweater, dangle
    earrings, hair ornament, smoked elk open-toe pumps.

EVELYN

ACT I—pink print dress, white sandal heels, necklace, apron, clip-on earrings, script. (Clothes should read as costume for movie within play.)

ACT II: Same.

CAPPY

ACT I—Hawaiian print shirt, khaki shorts, white socks, white sneakers, watch, belt.

ACT II—Hawaiian print shirt, khaki pleated pants, same accessories.

BOB

ACT II—black linen slacks, white shirt, sea green double breasted jacket, burgundy tassled dress shoes, black print socks, watch, black/burgundy tie, black belt.

PROPERTY PLOT

FURNITURE (Built into set)

Bed (5ft – 6ft. long, 5ft. wide)
Sofa (7ft long (2–4ft sections, 2 ft wide arm on SR side)
Counter behind sofa (8" wide fits along the back of sofa)
Table & seat (Booth style) (3'4" x 3' x 2'10")
Sink (practical)
Counter tops and cabinets
Refrigerator (practical)
Stove
Microwave
Bar Shelves

FURNITURE (Free standing)

Swivel chair
Director's chair (high stool)

Cellular phone
Coffee maker (practical) with 10 cups water and pack of
    Decaf coffee
4 mugs
1 mug with coffee stirers
Corkscrew
Sm. hand towel on counter
Horse ad in yellow envelope
Wine and water glasses
Tissue box
Lg. towel
Towel (in bathroom door)

Wine bottle (w/wine)
Pint of milk
Apple juice
Bag of cookies
Flowers in vase
Newspapers
4 magazines
3 newspapers and sports magazines
Sm. portable TV
Stack of mail
Bowel of fresh fruit
Make-up kit (w/lipstick, 4 shadows, lg. red pencil, 2 sponges, brown eyebrow pencil, 4 brushes, white lip brush, white pencil, pencil sharpener, powder & puff, extra sponges, extra tissues, cotton swabs)
Pack of cigarettes
Puppet of monster
Ladies briefcase
Envelope with clippings
Compact and lipstick
Red pen
Notebook
Tape recorder
Man's briefcase
1 bagel
2 rolls of paper towels
2 bottles of spring water
2 yogurts
Orange
Script
Clipboard
Pen

Walkie-talkie

The set is dressed with food supplies that are not used. The
    bed is fully made up. The windows have mini-blinds.
    The floor is carpeted. There are practical lamps in the
    bedroom area and the ceiling has track lighting.

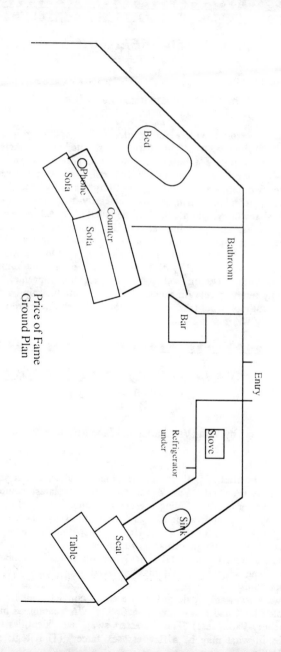

Price of Fame
Ground Plan

Bed

Phone

Sofa

Sofa

Counter

Bathroom

Bar

Entry

Stove

Refrigerator
under

Sink

Seat

Table

WHAT THE BELLHOP SAW
(Little Theatre)
(FARCE)

by Wm. Van Zandt and Jane Milmore

8 male, 4 female

The play starts with a rather nice fellow checking into a $400.00 suite in "New York City's finest hotel". From there it snowballs into a fabulous nightmare involving a Salman Rushdie-type author, an Iranian Terrorist, a monstrous shrew-like woman, a conniving bellboy, a monumentally incompetent F.B.I. man, a nubile celebrity-mad maid, a dim-witted secretary, and a cute little pigtailed girl. All the while, gag lines are popping at Orville Redenbacher speed. Everything happens at pretty much whirlwind velocity. This latest farce by Van Zandt and Milmore combines topical humor with the traditional antics of farce: doors slamming, characters careening and confusion reigning supreme. A wildly funny farce! An excellent piece of workmanship by our two authors who take pride in the old-fashioned craft of comedy writing. #25062

◆◆◆◆◆◆◆◆◆◆◆◆◆◆◆◆◆◆◆◆◆◆◆◆◆◆◆◆◆◆◆

THE SENATOR WORE PANTYHOSE
(Little Theatre)
(COMEDY)

by Wm. Van Zandt and Jane Milmore

7 male, 3 female

If you're tired of political and religious scandals, this is your greatest revenge! Van Zandt & Milmore's latest comedy revolves around the failing Presidential campaign of "Honest" Gabby Sandalson, a regular guy whose integrity has all but crippled his bid for the White House. Desparate for votes, his sleazeball campaign manager trumps up an implausible sex scandal which accidentally backfires on PMS Club leader Reverend Johnny and his makeup-faced wife Honey Pie; an opportunistic innkeeper with a penchant for antique food; the town's wayward single girl; two escaped convicts looking for stolen loot; and newscaster Don Bother. "A guaranteed hit!" (Asbury Park Press) "The characters swap beds, identities and jabs in what may be a flawless sex farce." (The Register). #21084

MIXED FEELINGS
(Little Theatre—Comedy)

Donald Churchill
m., 2 f., Int.

This is a riotous comedy about divorce, that ubiquitous, peculiar institution which so shapes practically everyone's life. Arthur and Norma, ex-spouses, live in separate apartments in the same building. Norma has second thoughts about her on-going affair with Arthur's best-friend; while Arthur isn't so sure he wants to continue *his* dalliance with Sonia, wife of a manufacturer with amusingly kinky sexual tastes (Dennis—the manufacturer—doesn't mind that his wife is having an affair; just so long as she continues to provide him with titillating accounts of it while he is dressed as a lady traffic cop). Most of Sonia's accounts are pure fiction, which seems to keep Dennis happy. Comic sparks are ignited into full-fledged farcical flames in the second act, when Dennis arrives in Arthur's flat for lessons in love from the legendary Arthur! "Riotous! A domestic laught romp! A super play. You'll laugh all the way home, I promise you.'—Eastbourne News. "Very funny ... a Churchill comedy that most people will thoroughly enjoy."—The Stage. Restricted New York City.

THE DECORATOR
(Little Theatre/Comedy)

Donald Churchill
m., 2 f., Int.

Much to her surprise, Marcia returns home to find that her flat has not been painted, as she arranged. In fact, the job hasn't even been started yet. There on the premises is the housepainter who is filling in for his ill colleague. As he begins work, there is a surprise visitor--the wife of the man with whom Marcia is having an affair, who has come to confront her nemesis and to exact her revenge by informing Marcia's husband of his wife's infidelity. Marcia is at her wit's end about what to do, until she gets a brilliant idea. It seems the housepainter is a part-time professional actor. Marcia hires him to impersonate her husband, Reggie, at the big confrontation later that day, when the wronged wife plans to return and spill the beans. Hilarity is piled upon hilarity as the housepainter, who takes his acting *very* seriously, portrays the absent Reggie. The wronged wife decides that the best way to get back at Marcia would be to sleep with her "husband" (the house painter), which is an ecstatic experience for them both. When Marcia learns that the housepainter/actor/husband has slept with her rival, she demands to have the opportunity to show the housepainter what *really* good sex is. "This has been the most amazing day of my life", says the sturdy painter, as Marcia leads him into her bedroom. "Irresistible."—London Daily Telegraph.

Other Publications for Your Interest

SOCIAL SECURITY
(LITTLE THEATRE—COMEDY)

By ANDREW BERGMAN

3 men, 3 women—Interior

This is a real, honest-to-goodness hit Broadway comedy, as in the Good Old Days of Broadway. Written by one of Hollywood's top comedy screenwriters ("Blazing Saddles" and "The Inlaws") and directed by the great Mike Nichols, this hilarious comedy starred Marlo Thomas and Ron Silver as a married couple who are art dealers. Their domestic tranquility is shattered upon the arrival of the wife's goody-goody nerd of a sister, her up-tight CPA husband and her Archetypal Jewish Mother. They are there to try to save their college student daughter from the horrors of living only for sex. The comic sparks really begin to fly when the mother hits it off with the elderly minimalist artist who is the art dealers' best client! "Just when you were beginning to think you were never going to laugh again on Broadway, along comes *Social Security* and you realize, with a rising feeling of joy, that it is once more safe to giggle in the streets. Indeed, you can laugh out loud, joyfully, with, as it were, social security, for the play is a hoot, and better yet, a sophisticated, even civilized hoot."—NY Post.   (#21255)

ALONE TOGETHER
(LITTLE THEATRE—COMEDY)

By LAWRENCE ROMAN

4 men, 2 women—Interior

Remember those wonderful Broadway comedies of the fifties and sixties, such as *Never Too Late* and *Take Her, She's Mine*? This new comedy by the author of *Under the Yum Yum Tree* is firmly in that tradition. Although not a hit with Broadway's jaded critics, *Alone Together* was a delight with audiences. On Broadway Janis Paige and Kevin McCarthy played a middle aged couple whose children have finally left the nest. They are now alone together—but not for long. All three sons come charging back home after experiencing some Hard Knocks in the Real World—and Mom and Dad have quite a time pushing them out of the house so they can once again be *alone together*. "Mr. Roman is a fast man with a funny line."—Chr. Sci. Mon. "A charmer."—Calgary Sunday Sun. "An amiable comedy . . . the audience roared with recognition, pleasure and amusement."—Gannett Westchester Newsp. "Delightfully wise and witty." Hollywood Reporter. "One of the funniest shows we've seen in ages."—Herald-News. TV.   (#238)